LONGING FOR YOU

The Journey from Intercession to Intimacy

Debra-Louise Cossu

Longing For You
by Debra-Louise Cossu

Printed in the United States of America

ISBN 9781600341342

www.xulonpress.com

THIS BOOK IS DEDICATED TO YOU
WHO WILL LIVE IT

AMAZING LOVE

I HEARD YOUR VOICE WHISPER MY NAME
I CLOSED MY EYES TO HIDE THE PAIN
YOUR STEADFAST GAZE WOULD NOT BE TURNED
AMAZING LOVE WITHIN YOU BURNED

YOUR HAND REACHED OUT & MINE WITHDREW
I DID NOT KNOW WHAT LOVE COULD DO
YOU GENTLY DRIED MY YEARS OF TEARS
AMAZING LOVE REMOVED ALL FEARS

GRATEFUL FOR HOW LONG YOU STOOD
I GATHERED ALL THE STRENGTH I COULD
TO LOOK NOW IN YOUR TENDER FACE
AMAZING LOVE I TOO EMBRACE

A VISUAL PRELUDE

Look to see this scene with your heart. The bride is standing, dressed in readiness, waiting for the wedding to begin. She is looking out a bay window with her hand lifted, pulling back the curtain, hoping to catch a glimpse of the groom's arrival. Her eyes are wide opened, and although it is a misty dawn she peers into, no amount of clouds will cause her to sit back down.

"Longing" could be the name of this picture if put onto a canvas.

However the bride is not the center of attention as you look. It is the Bridegroom. Christ is standing behind her, and His hand is imposed over hers, pulling back the curtain. The sun is shinning from behind Him through the window so as to cast His shadow over the Bride, and tears are flowing down His face. Oh yes, the Bride is looking, but dear one, it is the Groom who is longing. Jesus is longing for you.

TABLE OF CONTENTS

FOREWORD

By Mike Bickle, Director,
International House of Prayer of Kansas City

I remember Debbie when she first came on staff at the House of Prayer in Kansas City in June of 2002. Not only does her pure white hair cause her to stand out, her face has this radiance that draws people to take a second look. One day I told her I had been watching her and that it was evident how much she loved Jesus. Her smile was the only response. It is obvious to see that Debbie loves people.

She radiates His love to those around her. She even greets the visitors with a big smile and vibrant heart. Many of the young people here go to her for prayer and encouragement since she participates in both the night and day watches. I found out that she had been praying for my family since 1990. She knew us before we met her because of praying for us all those years. It is a joy to know her now as well. The leadership team here loves her, and we are so glad she is a part of the IHOP Missions Base.

The primary call on my life is to be an intercessor. Debbie's book, "Longing for You," is confirmation that others are realizing what a joy it is to live a lifestyle of prayer. The reality of going from intercession to intimacy" has occurred in her heart. It can happen in yours as well. She has written in such a simple and authentic style that the Voice of Love she listens to, can be heard clearly.

As I read, there was a quickening that made me want to turn the page and go on this journey from intercession to intimacy that she describes in a unique way. The heart of romance that beats in God for us is heard clearly. The reality of God's word is expressed in a concise manner, and in a tone of normal conversation, that caused me stop and talk to God as I read.

Reading the previews for each section caused me to want to read more. The review scriptures, the list of the names of God, and "Refuting Ungodly Beliefs", will help you explore your own personal journey from intercession to intimacy. The analogy of a bride being carried over the threshold will cause anticipation in you to experience each of these movements in your own heart as well.

I could envision the scenes vividly described of Esther, and Mary, and when Jesus bled. The description of the Bridegroom longing over the Bride brought tears to my eyes. It is a true representation of the Lord's heart for you.

Jesus really loves you. He is longing, for you. This book will cause you to long for Him more, just as it did me.

ACKNOWLEDGEMENTS

I acknowledge Jesus as the Lord of my life, and as Lord of all.

To each of my children, I acknowledge my love for you that grows daily. You are gifts from God in my heart. It is because of my love for you I am so determined to *really* learn how to pray!

INTRODUCTION

• Your life, your true life, begins at the cross

• A life of communion with Him will nourish you in love

• Now you can enjoy life with Him every day

• Your life will become intercession as you behold Jesus

• Romance is in His blood

• You were made for love

• Today is an important day

• He really makes all things new...that means all things

• This book is all about Him

• This book is all about you

• This book is about all of mankind

LONGING FOR YOU

Y ou are here by invitation. You have answered "yes" to the call of prayer.

Learning to pray is not developing a skill, but rather discovering a Person. His name is Jesus. As you read this book you will find yourself alone with the Lover of your soul. You will not want there to be any interruptions once you begin your journey inside these pages.

Therefore, the scripture references that unlocked these heart notes as each chapter unfolds will all be found in the back of the book for you to review and mediate upon. Also there you will find a list of a few Names of God I have come to know Him by. These will inspire you to search for other names that will become special to you as you come to know Him more each day.

For your consideration there is also a section refuting ungodly beliefs. Even some in the church claim such statements to be true, yet their basis cannot be found anywhere in the Bible. False realities will be dismantled as the truth of His love fills your heart.

I was introduced to Jesus as a teenager, but even before that had often found myself "praying" to God due to the circumstances of life. Now I spend many hours each day simply being with Him, which I find is the most enjoyable type of prayer. My definition of prayer is simply bringing together heaven and earth, in the will of God.

Currently I am a full time Intercessory Missionary at the International House of Prayer in Kansas City. From the secret place of prayer I get to first of all minister to Jesus in worship and adoration. After that, my prayers not only touch the lives of those I love, but have an impact on the nations of the earth as well. You will find more information about this place also in the back of the book.

I often feel like a mobile house of prayer while away on a mission trip across the world, and sometimes even just going to the local grocery store. I carry Him with me everywhere. I am drawn to those who have never before known His love, or are longing to experience it in a deeper way. This wonderful life has changed my perspective of what prayer really is, and I have been learning to pray for over 37 years.

I love to take what He pours in, and share it with everyone who will listen.

The first title in my heart for this book was, "Across the Threshold".

The years have progressed and the romance grown. When I went to write that here it came out,

"A Cross, the Threshold."

Our life, our true life, begins at the cross where Christ died.

He longs for you more than can be imagined in your heart. From the place of the cross you will get such a clear view of love, that everything else will gain a new perspective as well.

All of history finds its meaning at the foot of the cross, and so will you.

"Longing for You" clearly became the title of this book as I sat before the cross to gain His heart

for those who would be reading it.

It is Jesus who invited you personally to begin this journey.

This adventure of learning how to pray will bring you face to face with the One who is the answer to every prayer ever prayed, even when tears were the only words. He became flesh. He not only understands what is going on in your life, but will help you know what to do about it.

He really cares so much.

Go again and again to the foot of the cross. Longing for Him will increase with each visit, and you will then come to realize how much He longs for you.

A life of communion with Him will nourish you in love.

There are many books now written on intercession, which is simply a fancy word for prayer. I have no desire to write another. This book is about intimacy with the One who loves you more than any one else is able. This is a true story, and although I am sharing with you from mine, yours is being written, edited, and published daily.

We are like an opened book to all those around us. Our lives are a result and reflection of others who have brought us to this day. All things work together for the good for those who love Him and who are called according to His purpose.

All things! That really does mean ALL things.

This book is not one about inner healing or deliverance either. There are many resources available in those areas. God alone keeps accurate records of all our lives, and with much more detail than we have done, or anyone else for that matter.

The point to be settled here is that we alone are responsible for the responses of our heart to circumstances and relationships that touch our lives. There are times when we have had no control over what others have done. However, each of us dictates the condition of our hearts that result which help to set the foundation for the rest of our lives.

I attended a wedding that affected me like no other. As the groom speaks aloud his vows of love and devotion, he states, "I will NEVER divorce you." The bride included the same in hers. It was as if I could see lightening pierce throughout the room, penetrating with life all around.

Hope eternal flooded into the hearts of those who were there. I had come early as an intercessor to prepare the room and pray for those who would be attending. I am confident that the Love, which inspired that statement to be proclaimed out loud, touched hearts that were perhaps considering such a choice.

Jesus will never abandon you. He will never leave you. He loves you. He really loves you. He will always love you. He wants to be with you forever. You can enjoy life with Him every day. In His presence there is fullness of joy, regardless of the circumstances that surround you.

Your life will become intercession as you behold the Great Intercessor.

We become what we behold, and as you keep your eyes on Jesus, you will come to be just like Him. He is an intercessor. He is the Great Intercessor. He is at the Father's side right now praying for you as you read. An intercessor is one who stands in the gap, to bring together heaven and earth, according to the will of God.

He has invited you to partner with Him on the earth and see His Kingdom come. The desire to learn to pray has grown within your heart because your longing to know Him continues to grow stronger each day. Even in the dry seasons, it was longing for Him deep inside that drew you to this day of passion for His Presence.

He is also a lover, the greatest Lover of all.

Romance is in His blood.

Consider that statement for a moment. He died for you. He also lives for you and wants you to be with Him forever. Every movement of your heart towards Him caused Him to move a step closer, until finally, you were ready. Romance flows from inside of you as well. To love and be loved is not just a deep need, but the greatest of human joys.

You were made for love.

It used to be a dull ache resounding as an echo so far away, and out of your reach. Now you can feel it pulsing within as a mighty river. Like a Holy transfusion, new life is yours, quickening love with each heartbeat.

This is the day. Today is an important day. Actually there are two days that really matter. This day, and that day when you will see Him face to face, to give an account of every other. The past is over. Both the good and the bad really did happen. The facts cannot be changed. The future is not within your grasp, and only One sees it accurately.

Each of us has been granted another day of grace. What will you do with yours? Jesus Himself is looking at you with eyes of love. There is a divine exchange happening that you have been prepared for, and longed for, all your life.

Give Him your heart once again.

One more time, give Him your heart and let His love flood your being.

What you are feeling as you read is even now being inspired by the reality and the passion of His heart pouring into yours. The Spirit of Truth is by your side. The whisper of love resounding from heaven is silencing all other voices.

Listen well.

His love has been stored up and held as in a trust account to be released as soon as you desire it. What do you really want in this life? What is the longing that stirs so deep in your heart? What will satisfy the growing ache within?

Even as these words become blurry through your tears, you know He alone will satisfy.

Wave after wave of this love will continue, and not relent, until you respond to the longing of His heart towards you. Desire for His desire will now consume you. He has stood willing to pick you up, and at last you want to be. It is time to be set into the destiny prepared for your arrival.

There is no longer any reason to hesitate.

He will sustain the yes you now offer and nothing will ever be the same again.

He knew you two would meet in these pages.

Over and over He has stretched out His arms as they were that day on the cross, and set His gaze on you. Opened arms of love are now picking you up because yes, yes you are ready. He delights in you. He can't help it. Every time He stretches out His mighty hand, the One who was clothed in flesh sees the marks of love He will bear forever.

It's all about love.

He knows you far better than you know yourself. He loves you freely. You are His choice by desire, and He will never relent. He will never grow cold or withdraw His affection towards you. He has never been caught off guard or taken by surprise by your thoughts, or words, or actions, even when you were.

He, who knows it all, loves you the best. He never once turned away from you. He fashioned you individually, and likes everything about you. He wants to be with you.

He enjoys being with you.

He is with you even now.

Jesus makes all things new, and that really means ALL things.

The three steps, along the way in this journey of learning to pray, will be expressed through the analogy of a Bride being carried across the threshold.

The first scene is the Groom with delight, swooping up the bride into His arms.

This romance really is all about Him. Here we will learn who He is according to scripture.

As false realities are dismantled, the perceptions of man that developed outside of love will be removed, and you will experience a love never known before. Gaining under-standing of His part in this relationship leading to a life of prayer will help to fulfill yours. We love Him because He first loved us. Remind yourself of this every day over and over again.

He chose you long before you knew anything about Him.

The second scene is the Groom actually carrying the bride across the threshold. In this stage of the journey, you are the focus.

This romance really is all about you.

He has set His gaze upon you, and He wants you to see yourself as He does. He looks through lenses of love alone. The view of those around you has often been distorted by the portrait they have of themselves.

Learning who you really are brings clarity and new purpose as the days unfold. For this life of prayer to be an experience of joy and delight, it will take a daily decision to say "Yes" over and over again to simply being with Him.

You will begin to set aside personal times of communion with Him, and enjoy them.

Life makes it easy to forget who we are, if we ever really knew to start with.

He remembers with detail all the dreams in His heart for you. They will come to pass.

The third scene is where He is placing His bride back on her feet. He sets her down where she belongs, to do what she was created to do. This is where the fruit of love blossoms, as together you go forth to take the love that is shared, into the world.

This romance really is about all mankind.

As you become truly dependent upon Him, the freedom to stand in life, and in love, will change you forever. The desire for all to know Him will consume you like a living river of fire, and you will want to go out and tell the world about His love.

This book only contains 3 chapters. Praying is as easy as one, two, three, and yet part of a mystery words can never explain.

What you will find contained in these pages is not describing a plan or program, it's all about a Person.

You will be peering into the reality of Christ within, the hope of glory.

As you come to believe at last that your life really is hidden in His, you will live like never before. Those inside the church walls, and those who never have entered, will all be transformed by the love they will see in you. Because you did say, "Yes" to His proposal of love, you have already begun to learn to pray. Now nothing will ever be the same again, not even you!

If you are willing, if you dare, turn the page and come on the journey from intercession to intimacy that will transform your life forever!

CHAPTER ONE

- He has set His heart on you and proposed more than once

- Nothing is hidden from His gaze

- He bends over the balcony of heaven to listen to you

- Truth does set free, and He wants you to be free indeed

- He wants to put you on display for the glory of His Name

- Jesus is longing for you...look and you will see Him

- He speaks the invitation, "Come."

- You have His attention

- Ask and He will answer

- No one on earth can take your place in His heart

- Seeing angels did not satisfy...she had to see Jesus

- Prayer involves more than just you speaking to God

- This is your time for love

- He is looking for voluntary lovers...and here you are

- Yours is to be a life full of wonder from now on

- He chose you before you were in your mother's womb

- He is your destiny

- Today you are held in His arms

- You believe again

- You are a lover of God

- Forever He will bear the marks of love for you

- He is the answer

- All He has done...He has done for love

- Jesus wants you to know His will

- He is the defense of your life

- He's all around you

- He understands the emotional deluge within

- His peace will sustain you

- The cross must remain the center

- Everyone who came to Jesus was healed

• Continue to look into His eyes of love

• From the cross He proclaimed, "It is finished"

• You are resting where you belong...in His arms

• He is Lord of all

• The broken pieces of your life are connected by His love

• He does not want to remain as an intimate stranger

He picks you up as you leap off the ground.

You have been chosen, and finally believe that what is happening is real. His love is not a fairy tale and involves much more than castles in the sky. You are one He reached for from the cross, now lifted into His arms.

He chose you to be His own long ago and finally you believe it's true.

He set His heart on you and proposed more than once.

He had to have you.

He told His Father you were His desire.

He asked for you to be with Him where He is. He did everything that was necessary for that to happen. He came in person to claim you as His very own. He is a relentless Lover. He knew this day would come.

It was love for you that caused Him to cling to the cross.

He won, and so have you this day.

Love wins every time.

He holds you close with delight. There is no fear or doubt remaining within. You can see your reflection clearly in His eyes. His love casts away all fear. You are growing more confident in love with every breath.

Nothing is hidden from His gaze.

He chose you to be His very own. He wants you to bear His name forever. This romance has begun to transform every area of your life. You are awakening to a joy never known before. You really are different inside. This is more than a feeling. You know emotions can change with the weather, and yet somehow believe this love will always remain the same.

There is new strength and a stabilizing factor within that holds you secure, even as He is holding you now. At times, looking into the mirror with amazement, you wonder who the person smiling back could be. Soon you will discover the answer to that question. As you come to know the Lover of your soul more and more, you will see Him as He really is.

The clearer you come to see Him, the view you have of yourself will be changed.

You will begin to see yourself as He does.

He enjoys everything about you. Not only does He love you for real, He likes you so very much.

This chapter is all about Him. You will come to see Him, as He is, when you realize He looks through eyes of love at you. He delights in mercy that is new every morning. His mercy is much greater than any human weakness in you or anyone around you.

He bends over the balcony of heaven to listen to your voice, to hear the heart cry you cannot seem to put into words.

No one on earth really knows you. Not the real you deep inside. Not really. Not like He does. And even those who know you the best have not seen you as He does every moment. He formed and fashioned you individually.

There is none like you because there is none like Him, and you are made in His image.

Even if you have an identical twin, they really are not exactly like you. Perhaps you have fooled people at times pretending to be each other, but both of you know the ocean of difference between you that no man can see.

All that has not been uttered from the very depths of your being resounds in His heart, and He listens carefully. He has heard the weak and wavering "Yes" you offered to Him this day. The Bible tells us we love Him because He first loved us. This gift of first love caused you to leap with joy, to leap into His outstretched arms, at last.

He really is your first love, and wants to be first in your life from now on.

Already you have begun to believe this book is going to be full of things you long to hear, that you need to hear, and that are not often spoken aloud in the business of life. You are correct. Then even those things that appear at first glance to cause tears to flow freely shall become a healing balm that will restore your soul.

Truth does set free, and He wants you to be free indeed!

Suffering will reap a harvest of joy when placed in the hands of the One who not only created you, but delights in creating you anew. This is about a divine exchange. As you give Him your heart, somehow, His begins to beat within the depths of your very being.

You are getting to know the Lover of your soul and new life has begun…again.

Over and over, as often as you choose to accept, He will do what only He can. He delights in making all things new.

Every time the sun comes up you are being granted a brand new day full of promise.

Even the darkest night is swallowed up by the dawn. Sometimes it is cloudy all around, but the sun that shines from behind the clouds will not be hidden forever.

Light shines into the darkness, not the other way around. When you open up the curtains at night, the light from within goes out, darkness cannot come inside no mater how dark it is.

The light of His love will illuminate both the realities of the past and the imaginations about the future, granting you peace of mind that will guard your heart.

As you begin to see Him like never before, the light of His love will cause whatever you are facing to become clearer. You are experiencing the reality of His love right now, and beginning to get a new perspective of everything. In this chapter we are learning about Him. Even the views and paradigms you have of yourself will change as you look through His eyes of love.

The way His love affects you will be presented in a way you can neither deny nor refute ever again. Real beauty for ashes adorns you. He has clothed you in the splendor of holiness.

Holy to the Lord is written over your life.

He wants to put you on display for the glory of His Name.

He wants the world to know His love, and they will see it through your life. As you discover more about Him and how His heart beats for you, there will be a residue of love left everywhere you go. Listen carefully to His voice, and then when you open your mouth others too will hear Him speak.

Jesus is longing for you!

Look and you will see Him. Whenever you look to find Him, you will realize He has been looking at you all the time. His eyes are on you and He wants you to know it. Perhaps you will even blush as you look, but His gaze will not be turned away. He wants to be with you all the time, wherever you are, no matter what is going on.

There is a story of Queen Esther found in the Bible that is a glimpse of the confidence in love you are beginning to walk in. She had to make an appeal to the king. An important request needed to be made. Many lives depended on what she would say. The law in that day stated no one could go in to see the king without being summoned. If he wanted to speak with you, the king would extend his scepter when you entered, and you could draw near. If he did not want to hear your voice, you would be killed!

The process was that simple.

Esther had listened to the king share his heart many times. She knew how he ran his kingdom.

However, she had grown up as part of another Kingdom before coming into her position as Queen. Therefore, she was preparing for this visit in the way she knew would really make a difference. She prayed and fasted and had others join in with her as well. Only then was she confident enough to go and speak her heart to the king. Praying and fasting had prepared her heart to open her mouth.

Then, she got dressed and simply stood still.

She was aware that every day he looked over to see if he could catch a glimpse of her. He was enthralled with her beauty, which is a recorded fact. But more than that had happened in his heart. Because she had taken the time to discover his preferences and desires when getting ready to meet him the very first time, she was the one picked to be Queen. That night she was taken into not just his chambers, but deep into his heart.

All that she learned about him had caused him to want to be with her, and he knew she wanted to be with him. She understood who he was and knew what he liked. She cared about the things that were important to him, and let him know. She wanted this meeting to count just as much as the very first time they were together. It had to. Everything in the natural seemed to be in place, but it was her lifestyle of prayer and fasting that made the eternal difference that day.

The presumptions made here might not have occurred behind the scenes in their story, but even more intimate stirrings are happening now between you and the One who holds out His scepter in your direction.

Jesus, who chose you to be His own, wants to hear all you have to say, even when you have no words to offer. Nothing escapes His loving gaze. He is looking at you and beckons you to come closer.

He speaks the invitation, "COME".

Already you can see that learning to pray actually teaches you about the One to Whom you are praying. Nothing, no request, will be beyond your reach as you come closer to the One who alone can answer. You have found favor, and He has invited you into His chambers...the chambers of His heart.

He wants to share the secrets of His heart with you, and you now long to know them as well.

You ravished His heart even before your first glance in His direction.

Therefore, now, what is your petition? What do you desire for yourself and for those you love? What is your further request for the world beyond?

You have His attention. Ask, and He will answer.

You will not be able to contain all the love that He offers.

It will seem like too much, yet never really become enough.

Longing is His gift to you. You will soon be pouring into the lives of those around you, but for now He is pouring into you. Christ lives in you. Think about that. Believe it, and then live like it just for today, as long as today remains.

His fervent desire is for you. He is the Great Intercessor, and is praying for you right now. Suddenly you will become aware of the answers to prayer that have brought you to this day. You are discovering that living a life of prayer is really about saying, "Yes" to a life of love.

Oh indeed, this is a love story. It is your story to tell from now on!

The One, who holds the universe in the palm of His hand, is never too busy to hold you. He who calls every star by name, also named you. It is true that your earthy parents wrote the name that appears on your birth certificate, but He knew you long before they were even born. Let this truth flood your heart. He calls you by name. Not only did He name you, He wants you to know you are His favorite.

There is not one on earth who can take your place in His heart.

As you come to believe you are His favorite you will start to meet others who think they are as well. You will realize just as a parent can convince each child they are so special, God wants to convince you of the same. He wants you to know for sure how much He loves you. He loves you intimately, in all the uniqueness that is yours alone.

He loves you more than any earthy parent is able. Love begets love, and as your heart begins to return His love you will come to believe how much Jesus really loves you. "Jesus Loves Me" is not just a song for children, but a song of love for you.

There is another glimpse of how one who loves Him affects His heart in the gospel of John. The scene is after Jesus had been laid in the tomb, and Mary comes back for one more look and to end to what still needed to be done for His burial. She loved Him because she knew He really loved her. Jesus had just died on the cross and retrieved the keys of death and hell. He loosed those held captive, and accomplished all kinds of other spiritual matters that remain a mystery this day.

Then as He was on His way back where He belonged, to His Father's side in glory, He took a side trip.

Mary loved Him so much that He could not leave her crying in such despair. She was outside the tomb weeping and stooped down to look inside. She saw two angels where the body of Jesus had lain.

Seeing angels did not satisfy her…she had to see Jesus.

She begins to pour out her heart about how she had to find Him, and suddenly Jesus is standing before her. She does not recognize Him at first though…until He could no longer contain Himself, and called her by name. At that moment, her heart exploded with joy, for no one said her name the way He did. Jesus had to ask her not to cling to Him because He had not yet gone to see His Father.

She was to go and tell the others, "He is alive". She went willingly to tell of His resurrection. Now, more than ever before, she was confident in love and would go anywhere He asked and would speak whatever He wanted her to say.

That same day He came back and stood in the midst of where the disciples had gathered. He had to come back the very same day! He is waiting now for another day when He will come again, which is the message you will begin to proclaim with new clarity and joy, because you have heard Him call your name as well.

He delights in mercy and is not willing for anyone to perish. Your desire to learn to pray has caused you to love Him more. Soon you too will go to tell everyone that He is alive. You will declare that He really loves them, because you know now how much He loves you.

As you declare His word, Jesus will confirm it. He only requires from you that which He alone can supply. He is the Living Word. The Bible is one way He speaks to us today.

He reveals Himself through the written word. You will learn more about Him by reading the Bible than any other book attempting to describe Him.

You will discover soon the importance of speaking (praying) the word back to Him. As we simply tell Jesus what He told us to tell Him, somehow in the economy of God, prayer occurs that will not be deigned. That fervent and effective prayer is birthed, that causes angels and demons to move, and lives to be changed forever.

With a simple desire of learning how to pray, suddenly you have found yourself in love. Whatever a life of prayer means, you know you will get to spend time with Him, and that is now a consuming passion. You do want to learn to pray for those you love effectively. Things happening in the world are moving your heart as well, and you feel you have to pray about them. This hunger for His Presence is answering your own personal heart cry to hear His voice.

Now you are sure that prayer involves more than just you speaking to God.

You no longer have to wonder if He is listening to you. That was settled when He picked you up in response to the weak, and still at times wavering, "Yes" you offered.

You know He hears your voice, even when you cannot utter a word.

Now you realize that He wants to speak to you as well.

He wants to share the secrets of His heart with you.

He wants a partner in this life who listens to the concerns of His heart, and who will listen with their heart to what He has to say. He chose you. He is delighted with your renewed passion for Him. Even without full knowledge of the depth of the "Yes" you have declared, there is a resolve within that no matter what the cost, this time, this time, you will remain in His arms.

This is your time for love.

In abandonment you are ready for the journey, wherever He will take you.

You feel so safe. Peace at last is yours. There is a joy and excitement you have never known as each morning dawns. Each new day is now a gift of love, of discovery, of fulfillment. Even when the clouds of adversity and disappointment come to hide His beautiful face, you see beyond what is visible, and look up until you can catch His gaze set lovingly upon you.

Searching into the night, and seeing nothing at all, will never be able to rob you of believing again. He is extravagant in His love, and determined to win all of your heart. The kindness of His heart continues to overwhelm you. His goodness is swallowing up all that has not been good..He is looking for voluntary lovers, and here you are.

Your gaze is locked with His, and you are beginning to see Him as He really is.

His love for you, that cannot be refuted by any man or circumstance ever again, is coursing through your being like a river full of life. Your heart is flooded with the truth of His love, and you are free at last to love Him in return.

All the years of waiting to find true love are suddenly swallowed up in this moment because He holds you close. You wanted to answer His call to you before, to be able to respond, to finally believe, but until now too many other things were grasping for your attention.

Some of those things will not go away, and some people you must give attention to for a long time, but not at this moment.

Right now, He is all that matters.

Finally, you are resting in His strength, held secure in His arms.

Everything else will take its rightful place, because now you are where you belong. You have said, "Yes" to His incredible proposal of love. A life of love, and a love that will last for all of your life, is no longer an empty ache within.

There is another feeling, now increasing, more like the one that comes from laughing so hard, that you have to hold your tummy as tears come pouring down your face. You think you need to stop being so loud. You try to catch your breath. Your face becomes as red as the first time you blushed when realizing the one you loved was looking at you in the same way.

Now again you have been found in love, and this joy cannot be contained. You want to continue laughing out loud regardless of the opinion of those around you. This reality of love seems too much to grasp, yet causes you to long for more.

His love is like no other.

It is full of joy unspeakable, and full of wonder.

Yours is to be a life full of wonder from now on.

His vow of love resounded from the cross.

It echoed through the corridors of time to become the whisper in your heart heard so clear this day. He is holding you close to Himself. You can almost feel the warmth of His breath upon your face. He really wants to speak to you personally, intimately, and heart to heart.

He chose you for love before you were in your mother's womb, and His love will carry you into eternity. Many things have occurred to bring you to this day, but you will see, it was truly all for love. The path set before you, He paved Himself.

Now is the time to focus on Him.

Discovering what will happen down the road is for another day. Today He wants your attention and your affection. He wants you to know all about Him, and to see Him as He really is. Held up in His arms you will have an eternal perspective never seen before.

Step by step the future will unfold, but today you see only into His eyes.

He is your destiny!

You can remember the events during your life when those arms scooped you up, and it was just in time. Perhaps unaware of the depth of your love, others turned and walked away from you. You believed your heart would break to pieces.

The rejection and abandonment fed a self-hatred far worse than was in the heart of any man towards you. They simply did not know how to love, and if they had remained in your life, as you so desperately desired, you would not know His love this day.

Maybe due to the sin of others, more than once, your physical life was even put into danger. What was proposed, as a pathway to possibly end your life, could not succeed. What was meant to at least harden and destroy your heart, actually led to the awakening desire within for you to really live, to really love, to be held as you are this day.

Painfully perhaps you also remember the times you struggled free to go another way than the one He was headed in. Stop. Stop being so hard on yourself. Refocus your attention and look to see the One who loves you like no other is able. Remember "Jesus Loves Me" is now a love song resounding from your heart. It is the reality that will hold and keep you for this One who sings over you with joy.

Today you are held in His arms.

You are leaning upon your Beloved, and now so close to Him, that nothing else matters. This is a new day. This is the day. You have said, "Yes" to His love. You jumped up when He lifted you off the ground. The becoming one forever is all that matters.

You are now sure nothing will ever separate you from Him.

You believe again.

You are getting to know Him, not just learning more facts or opinions.

You have begun to really trust. Your heart feels safe with Him. Discovering how much He really loves you, and how faithful He will always be, is the foundation of a life of prayer. As you listen to hear His voice, as you feel His heartbeat so strong, thanksgiving and devotion will overflow the previously set boundaries of your own heart.

Then, at last, the natural exchange of words back and forth will form the prayers that will bring answers for you and many others as well.

Jesus is the Great Intercessor, and as you get to know Him, you will learn the language of love that is called prayer.

One of His own prayers is recorded in the gospel of John. John is the disciple who called himself so often, "the one that Jesus loves", that others called him that as well! There it is again, the confidence in love that comes from believing He loves you personally.

And because you now know you too are the one He loves, you have truly become a lover of God.

There is a dividing line being drawn in this generation... God lovers and God haters. No one will be able to remain in between opinions for much longer. You really are fully convinced of His love now, and yours grows stronger for Him day by day.

You are a lover of God because you now believe He loves you.

When Jesus was talking to His Father (praying) in John's gospel, He declared that He wanted you to be with Him. He was clothed in garments of skin so that could happen. Today He comes to dwell in you. Christ in you is called the hope of glory. He lived on earth in a human body.

He experienced real pain, and real blood was spilled out, for you.

And now He is in a heavenly body, but it is a body nevertheless. He could tell His disciples to look and see His hands and His feet, and to put their hand into His side, because He had become flesh in order to hang on the cross.

Forever He will bear these marks of love.

Love for you, and for all who believe, and for all who have yet to believe in His love as well, walked upon the earth as a man. In this recorded prayer Jesus first prayed for Himself. He was confident in love and knew His Father cared about what was on His heart. Love is the foundation of all prayer that will be answered.

Then He prayed that you would be with Him...and here you are!

After praying for you, He included those who would get to know Him because of your testimony of love. He wants you to be as confident in love as He is. Because you are already growing in the reality of love to a new degree, you have found yourself held in His arms today.

The book of Revelation proclaims that He was slain, and tells us of a scene in heaven celebrating this fact. We read that there are myriads of angels, 24 elders, and 4 really interesting creatures described that worship Him continually. They do not have divided hearts, hidden agendas, or the cares of this life to distract them.

Yet at one point He looked past them, and set His gaze upon you.

You are not an accident or an inconvenience.

Your name is carved upon His hands.

He is your Creator.

The Psalms speak all about life on earth and the various seasons that occur in the human heart. Read them and discover that what you are going through has an answer of love.

He loves you, just as you are right now.

He sees you complete in Him, and day-by-day, you will come to know this is true.

A life of prayer cannot be taught, no matter how hard you try to learn. It cannot be caught, no matter how desperately you try to grasp it from another. The only way to have a life of prayer is to seek the One who has invited you to discover the depths of His love. He placed this desire inside of you to pray, so you could find Him.

Seek and you will find is true. Seek to pray, and you will find that your life in Him becomes the prayer.

Learning to pray will not occur through any formula or list or method or person you know. Prayers that send you on a search for the One, who alone can answer, is the answer. In His Presence you will be caught up to somehow learn lessons not found in any book. When you seek Him with all your heart, suddenly you will find yourself eye to eye with the Lover of your soul.

He is the answer.

He wants you to know He is the only answer to the longing of your heart.

In Ephesians there is a prayer that is prayed for you to know the love of Christ that surpasses knowledge, so that you may be filled up with all the fullness of God. This knowledge, the knowledge of His love, is the foundation of a life of intercession that is truly more intimate than any relationship on the earth.

You will discover, all that He has done, He has done for love.

When you were born again, your life became hidden in His.

You will only find lasting joy in life as you come to realize that this statement is true. Hope will override disappointment when you 'find yourself' in Him. You have been invited to know Him. To see Him as He really is. The over flow of worship and adoration in a life of devotion, will birth revelation that becomes only as clear as you desire it to be.

Jesus wants you to know His will.

You are learning to hear His voice. His is the voice of love, and it sounds different from all others. He does not have to shout for you to hear Him. His voice resounds above those that are raised to demand your attention. He also wants you know He listens to what you have to say, even when you cannot utter a word. From the depths of your soul you cried out to know Him, and He is answering that prayer right now.

Tears have been called liquid prayers, and He has gathered every one of yours.

Heaven has been arrested with the display of His love for you. He sat enthroned at the flood and remains on the throne today. It is safe to trust Him, to trust in His love.

Do not be afraid. He is your refuge.

He is your strength.

He is a very present help in time of trouble.

He is the defense of your life.

He's all around you.

What a mystery this is, you in Him and Him in you, then somehow He is all around you at the same time. He breaks the silence of the unknown by speaking into your heart. He begins revealing glimpses into mysteries you will long to search out all your life, and then peer into for all of eternity as well.

God expressed Himself in the face of Jesus when He became flesh. While clothed in garments of skin, He had to eat, sleep, and wrestle with human emotions like those described in the garden scene just before His crucifixion.

It was real blood that was shed for you. Life is in the blood, in THE BLOOD.

He is fully God and fully man. What does this mean! He wants to let you know.

He understands the emotional deluge from grief and sorrow and worry and fear.

The first time His precious blood was poured out was while in prayer preparing to go to the cross. Knowing of, yet not experiencing sin Himself, coupled with the reality of being separated from His Father's gaze for the first time since before time began, caused Him to sweat great drops of blood.

What was about to happen would change everything. He knew this was the only way to secure His Father's gaze upon you. He carried the anguish and torment of mental agony then, so now you do not have to. He understands when overwhelming thoughts consume your waking hours, and continue to rob you of sleep as well.

The next time they come to disrupt your mind and heart, you now know He paid for your peace.

His peace will sustain you. Those precious drops that flowed are part of the perpetual covenant of peace that is now yours. Peace is yours. Because you have come to know

Him, all that His blood bought for you can be applied to every area and circumstance and relationship.

Jesus also bled internally. He was bruised for the generations past. His blood overcomes those inherited tendencies within you called iniquity. At family reunions you might feel the same old you is still there, but after experiencing new life in your heart for real, the evidence of your salvation will appear so clearly that everyone will know there is something different about you.

You will know how to pray for those still trapped in their old nature, and lead them to life eternal here and now. He bled deep inside to make provision for what was given to you in the natural. How you can live in the supernatural. You have the power of His life within that overcomes the sinfulness of all mankind.

New life now causes His blessing to flow through you, and into all the generations yet to be. Getting to know Him involves this picture of what He endured for you, and there are five other ways He bled for you as well. Yes, romance is in His blood. The most effective prayers you pray will spring from the reality of His victory over sin and sickness. As you walk in the victory of the cross, those around you will begin to long for victory as well, and you can introduce them to the Victorious One.

You need to know and understand the seven ways Jesus bled because they are important springboards for almost any situation or person you will find yourself praying for. The blood He shed is the foundation of the freedom and joy that will accompany you in this life.

As you grow in this love relationship called prayer, the cross must remain the center.

he ways described in the Bible of how He bled are the two just mentioned of when He bled out of the sweat glands in His forehead, medically known as hematidrosis, and the internal bleeding that resulted from the bruises that developed when He was being slapped and hit and kicked. Then thirdly He was scourged on His back for your physical healing.

Everyone who came to Jesus in the gospels was healed. His answer was always, "Yes. Be healed". He heals all diseases, and forgives all sins. That is what the Bible says, and it is spoken in the present tense. It is always His will to heal. His answer today is "Yes". His answer to you is "Yes".

At the cross that issue was settled.

As you continue to look into His eyes of love you will know this is true.

There are mysteries in life, and Christians will continue to die until the day He returns, but it should not be of sickness. Do not be drawn away into argument or opinion right now. Ask to see the stripes on His back, and then try to tell Him it was not enough. His blood secured both salvation for your soul, and healing for your body.

He would never tell you He wants to teach you a lesson, and then refuse to save you. Nor would He say that He would get more glory by not answering your heart cry for salvation, and then send you to hell. Never! The glory of the cross is your eternal salvation, and healing for your body today. Ask Him. I am praying for healing in hearts, and bodies, of all who read this book. His love, poured out in His blood, is victorious. He knew what it meant on that day, when from the cross

He proclaimed, "It is finished".

You can live in the fullness of all those words mean today.

The fourth time His blood flowed when the crown of thorns was placed upon His brow. This was meant to mock His Kingship, challenging Him as Lord. This portion of His blood covers when you have placed anything, or anyone, in the position He alone can fill in your life. Everything that exalts itself above Christ in your life is a point of sin and will keep you from being held in His arms.

You have given your heart to Him more than once, and taken it back just as often. Over and over He picked you up as soon as you cried out for Him to come. The other things in life, and the relationships that kept you out of His arms, will not sway you away any more.

Enough is enough, and His blood is enough!

You are resting where you belong, in His arms.

The fifth time He bled was when His hands were pierced through for the evil things you have done. His blood atones for everything. There is no sin more powerful than His blood. Now your hands can be instruments of righteousness. He wants to bless what you put your hands to.

Remember you are now holy unto the Lord.

The sixth time He bled was when His feet were pierced through for when you walked in your own way. We are to be willing, and obedient. Actions flow from what is conceived inside the heart and mind before any steps are ever taken.

Renew your mind and heart with the scriptures and you will walk in His ways.

The seventh and last way He bled was when His side was pierced. He was wounded for the transgressions that resulted due to deliberate and willful rebellion. These are presumptuous sins from when you know better, but choose to pursue what is wrong. As you grow in love with this One who endured so much for the sake of love, for you personally, the fear of the Lord will both compel you in love, and constrain you from sin.

Sin will become as appalling to you as it is to Him whose name is Savior.

In Song of Solomon we are told His body is like carved ivory, inlaid with sapphires. The carving occurred with every strip and lash of the whip. His flesh was carved out to make a place for you, forever. The sapphires inlaid in the carved out places represent revelation. He felt real pain and poured out real blood.

He endured this agony, because of the revelation of love that caused Him to go to the cross, for you. He knew each mark was victory over sin that had separated you for too long. Now you will be together forever. You are worth it all to Him. He is your Savior, and His Name is a strong tower.

Loving Him as Savior will cause you to trust Him as Lord.

He is a safe haven where your heart can be anchored in peace.

He is Lord of all.

He is where you will find rest for your soul.

Discovering the different aspects of who He is can be accomplished as you embrace Him by the names in which He reveals Himself all through the scriptures. As you call Him by name, by whatever name you need Him to be, He will show Himself.

Because you have come to dwell in the chambers of His heart, you will see the different aspects of who He really is. Life circumstances will then be moved into a new perspective.

You will at times find yourself standing on tiptoe to get a closer look from His vantage point of Love, Love Eternal.

He will help you to lift your eyes above the waves pounding all around you long enough to catch His gaze. The storm winds will suddenly not seem as threatening as they were when you felt all alone. Jesus was broken to gather you into the deepest places of His heart.

The broken pieces of your life will be put back together with the mortar of His love.

You will fit properly into place as His love surrounds all the edges of your life. Those areas, which are rough, and those, which are worn, and those that just need a little more cushioning, will all be connected by His love. Like creating a beautiful stained glass window, He is at work, and moving piece by piece to put things together in love.

With tender hands He is arranging the seasons of your life according to the view He has seen when all is completed. His light and love will shine through your life as the beauty of His love adorns you.

His name is also Jealous.

His own zeal for you will perform the intentions of His heart.

You will lack no good thing. He shall supply all that you need from the bounty of His riches in glory that He longs to share with you. What He is asking you to do in this part of your journey of prayer is to be still and know…to know Him.

He does not want to remain any longer as an intimate stranger.

He gave His life for you to be with Him, and wants your life in return.

It is His kindness that has drawn you in and picked you up to be held as you are at this moment. You will find Him to be both the Lamb who was slain, and the Lion who is soon returning. The mystery of His love is to be unlocked as your heart opens up to His.

He wants to personally give you all the answers you long to know.

The 'work' of God for you is not for you to pray to Him, but for you to believe in Him. Then you will have answers not just for yourself, but also for those around you. Your conversations with Him will become the prayers you could never have prayed until this day.

What is required to live a life of prayer, is to come to know the One to whom you are praying. He is gracious and slow to anger. You did not do anything wrong by not having the kind of prayer life you longed for before now, you could not. Every tear, sigh, and inkling of your heart towards Him, brought you to this day.

It all counts for eternity.

You did what you knew to do.

Now He will do what only He is able.

His love is like a shoreless ocean. The ebb and flow of His love carried you until you were picked up in His arms.

The boundaries set by your own thoughts, and the opinions of others, will be washed away as you are held in the reality of His arms.

It is now time to be carried across the threshold called prayer.

CHAPTER TWO

- Now you are not just held, you are being carried

- You begin to look forward instead of behind you

- You are a God lover

- The real you now emerging is hidden in Him

- There is peace and joy in believing

- You were made for love

- You are the joy set before Him

- He will always love you

- You have to love yourself as He does to be able to love

- The righteous are bold as a lion

- One man or woman plus God equals a majority

- Only love will last

- The joy of the Lord is your strength

- The blush of love has covered over all shame

- Your life is His prayer and you have become His answer

- When you spoke "Yes" to Him the angels danced

- All of heaven rejoiced because He smiled

- This is a day of wonder

- This is your day of love

- You are alive

- Your life was spared

- You were made for love, and love wins every time

- There is nothing for you to do right now, but cling

- Long before time began, God dreamt a dream...YOU

- Today in quietness and confidence you have found rest

- There is no condemnation in love

- There is something bigger going on

- He is guarding you jealously

- You have developed a hunger for His will

- You now want all your days to count for eternity's sake

• Your heart is being expanded in the process

• This is the day

• You are free indeed

• You now look past what is visible to the cross

• You know pride is sin, and so is false humility

• Truth is truth, and the truth is, you are loved

• You are becoming one with Him

• All of His riches in glory are yours

• Tears were the precious seed that softened your heart

You are no longer just being held.
You begin to move forward.
Now you are being carried…in His arms of love.

He is holding you much closer, and as you feel the sway of His steps, everything seems to be changing. This is more than the stirring in your heart you have become so familiar with. You are still being held gently in His arms, but your grasp on Him has become Lighter. The safety and security of His nearness continues to calm you, and yet an unfamiliar expectancy is growing.

You begin look all around.

Everything seems so new.

You are not alone. You will never be alone again. You believe you can trust Him. He has proved His faithfulness. He is so strong. He will never drop you. In confidence you snuggle in and press closer to Him than you did when He first picked you up.

You begin to look forward instead of behind you.

Peace, a covenant of peace, is springing from His love.

The past has been taken care of, and there is hope for the future like never before.

You are leaning upon Him as the bride did in the Song of Solomon. Coming up out of the ashes of the past you are freed from the vain imaginations of your own thoughts. You now realize, that the false realties presented as truth for the rest of your life, cannot affect your heart ever again.

Although some things really occurred that you wish never had, there is a higher truth now, freeing you for that which is yet to be. You are not the same person you were yesterday, perhaps not even the same as an hour ago. Neither what you have done in the past, nor what you do from now on, can dictate the value of your life. It is not what you do, But who you are, that sets the plumb line for your future.

You are a God lover.

Lovers can produce much more than workers all the time.

You know now that His love cannot be earned. He will never Withhold His affections from you.

If you could earn His love, then perhaps you could lose it as well.

Neither opinion is true. The perspective you have of yourself is changing because of His love. None of the opinions of others will be able to sway the person you now see so clearly in the mirror.

Not now, not ever again.

There is only One who holds such a place of influence In your life. You have experienced that Christ living in you grants a wisdom you never had before. The questions of life are being answered.

You are beginning to discover that you, the real you now emerging, is hidden in Him.

The desire to belong is a basic human need. There are people you have come to identify with through family ties, church, work, and even your favorite hobby. Each one will remain special.

However now you realize the most important relationship you have is with Jesus.

Because you have found yourself in His arms, you are really finding yourself at last! You will begin to enjoy the hope of your calling. You have answered His call to prayer and a new hope is filling you.

There is peace and joy in believing. You will not be disappointed trusting in Him.

You have learned to listen to His voice, His voice of love.

Now those you speak to will hear His voice of love as well.

Love will permeate the very air around you. You were made for love.

You are adorned with His love.

He wants to put you on display.

He will show His glory through your life, from the secret place of your life together.

Pride has shut its mouth.

The boldness that only the righteous walk in is where He is taking you now. Confidence in love causes you to radiate with life. New life is blossoming in your heart. Joy is expanding the borders of who you are. The person you have always been, yet never knew existed, is emerging with every step you take held in His arms.

You are going across the threshold.

The Passover lamb was slain on the threshold in the story recorded in Exodus. Jesus is the Lamb that was slain from before the foundation of the world.

You already know He died for you. That is why you are now living for Him.

The One who exists outside of time, stepped into this world, just for a moment, so you could step into Him forever. As He watched His chosen people celebrate the first Passover meal, with joy He looked forward to the day He would go to the cross as the last, and only, sacrifice ever needed.

The last supper was indeed, the 'meal of His life'.

He told His disciples of His fervent desire in sharing that meal with them.

He knew what was about to happen, and had joyfully anticipated this event. He had given us a wonderful preview in the book of Exodus. He knew He was the Lamb that was slain, and the Bread of Life as well.

Life, not death, was the purpose of the cross.

He was peering through the lattice of time and saw you this very day.

You were the joy set before Him.

You are the joy set before Him now.

Joy caused Him to give up His life, so you would never die. Joy is now yours as well.

You are carried close to Jesus, and He will never let you go. Actually, you will never let Him go. Remember He is looking for voluntary lovers. You are free to go, but no longer want to be apart from Him ever again. Confidence in love caused you to run into His arms, and not away from Him as you did before when things occurred that made you to hide in shame.

He is Love Eternal. He will always love you.

Forever.

This journey of learning to pray is causing you to discover who you are.

Now you know that you are loved. Knowing that He loves you just as you are is causing you to love yourself as well. Realizing this, and declaring it, is not being prideful or self focused. For too long you have hated what He loves.

Remember, Jesus loves you.

As you come to love Him more, you will begin to love yourself.

You have to love yourself, as He does, to have love for anyone else.

All you are is because of Him and will cause a humility leading to dominion to flow through you. The righteous are bold as a lion. The humility leading to dominion takes you right back to humility that will cause you to inherit the earth.

The humble will inherit the earth, and you are about to step into your inheritance.

He is taking you where you could never go on your own.

Confidence is not pride, confidence is confidence.

Humility that gives way to the purposes of God occurs in those who are not wise in their own opinion. You have decided to believe Him and all that His love has proclaimed about you.

You will soon stand, and stand strong forever, in love.

Because the north winds of adversity and the south winds of blessing have blown over your life, and transformed your heart, you are being changed from glory to glory.

One man or woman plus God equals a majority.

He's doing a new thing in the earth, in you.

The Sermon on the Mount gives us a description of one who is blessed. The original word blessed means, happy, fortunate, and to be envied. You will be blessed as you embrace these character qualities in making your daily choices. They will result from a life of prayer, and lead you into a life full of love.

Jesus says you are blessed if you are poor in spirit, when you mourn, when you are meek, as you hunger and thirst for righteousness, when you are merciful, and pure in heart, and being a peacemaker, and when you are persecuted for righteousness sake.

Perhaps no one has ever approached you and made you such an offer before. You have become a part of a Kingdom that is not of this world. Remember there are divine exchanges going on all the time. He gives you His heart of love over and over when you give Him yours, in any condition, just once!

Life is all about love.

Only love will last.

Love is the only thing that will remain when all is said and done in this life. Did you learn to love? There is nothing else that you can present before the Throne of God. As the above responses become yours, instead of what the world says you should be like, not only will you be transformed, but all those around you will be as well.

As you seek Him, that which is important for a life of prayer will fall into proper perspective. You will grow in wisdom beyond your years as revelation from hearing His voice, and meditation on His Word, begin to transform your inner life. No longer can waves of iniquity toss you about. You are carried in arms of love every step of the way. You go forward leaning. Your weakness has been consumed by the power of His love.

You will rise up soon to take your place confident in love.

The joy of the Lord is your strength.

You are radiant.

The blush of love has covered over all shame.

Your life is His prayer, and you have also become His answer.

You are still being confirmed in His love, and your heart is now so overflowing, you begin to tell Him more and more that you love Him. He will truly circumcise your ears as He has done to your heart. Every time you try to tell Him how much you love Him, what will resound is still the reality of His love for you, but even louder now.

When you spoke "Yes" to His invitation of love, the angels danced.

All of heaven rejoiced, because He smiled.

He smiles over you this day, and from now on, you will smile at life.

You no longer have to just mouth the words of all things working together for your good. You really believe it is true. Yes, life can be hard, but He is so good. You do love Him, because you know He loves you. You are called according to His purpose and all of your personal agendas have been left behind. Everything that happened in your life, EVERYTHING, brought you to this day of being carried by Him.

He is taking you, into a new place, to live a new life.

The surrounding circumstances might not change right away, and perhaps never; but you have been changed forever. This is a day of wonder. This is a day of love. Now everyday is your day for love. There is no God like Him who works in behalf of the one who waits. You have waited for love, and He opened the heavens and came down to pick you up in this moment.

He now carries you close.

You know who He is from a whole new perspective, and are beginning to see yourself as He does. All the darkness of shame and condemnation, which life apart from love brought to you, will become like a black velvet cushion for your life.

You are like a multifaceted diamond. All the beauty of who you are can be seen clearly now because of every day it took to get you to this point. You would not be who you are, held so close to His heart, if your own heart had not been through all it has been.

You made it.

The perfect balance coming from different winds of adversity and trial and testing, were met with the right amount of gentle breezes containing His blessing, just like you are feeling right now. Both have been used to remove what had kept you out of His arms of love. When you said, "Yes" to His proposal of love, you chose life.

You are alive.

Your life was spared.

You will now live each day to the full.

This desire to learn to pray is the evidence that your heart still beats strong in love.

Neither time nor circumstance could harden your heart forever.

You were made for love, and love wins every time.

There were a few blockages that grew within the hardened places of your heart, and they had to be removed. That is what is occurring right now, they are being dissipated with love as you read. Time has been your friend. Since the first moment He picked you up, a grand reversal began, to soften and to cleanse, every part of your being.

He is taking the steps needed to get you across the threshold.

Along the way, some of the facts of your humanity will be highlighted again in your mind. However, this time, peace will suddenly prevail. Your heart has found its rest in love, and there you will stay. You will not be moved by turmoil any more.

Jesus gives rest to His Beloved.

Be still.

You know He is God.

There is nothing for you to do right now, but cling. Hold tightly to the One who will do all that is needed to be done. If God only helps those who help themselves, the cross is the biggest mockery of all, and His pain and suffering was needless. Surely it was your helplessness that caused you to trust the power of the cross.

You believe, like Mary, that His Resurrection occurred, and that He is alive today.

You are experiencing your own resurrection somehow with every step He takes.

You do believe God is good. There is no man on earth who is good by nature. We were all born in sin. But you have been born again. His goodness and mercy are now companions on either side as He carries you. There is a healing balm saturating your soul.

This romance has taken you from sincerity to intensity.

Long before time began God dreamt a dream, and you were brought forth.

Now all the hopes and dreams within you are coming to life.

He carried you in His heart long before you were picked up in His arms.

Now you have entered into His rest, and you know you are not dreaming.

This life of love is real life at last. Somehow your heart is more fully alert, awake, and alive, than ever before. Even the wise virgins fell asleep in the gospel story. You cannot slumber any more. There is something so different happening, and you do not want to miss anything. You won't.

As you move held in His arms, you realize this is the kind of peace that helps to open your eyes. Your eyes are now wide opened. You are beginning to have more and more awareness, and concern, for those around you.

Those you do not know, and some who are far away, are beginning to capture your heart. Jesus loves your enthusiasm, but for now you are the focus, no one else. You will have your day of going out.

You will go into new places you never even thought about before, and back to some places you had hoped to forget. One day others will be the focus, but for now it's all about you. You cannot save everyone any way and actually now realize you cannot save anyone. You have been redeemed, and everything in your life is now being transformed by this touch of amazing love found in a life of prayer.

Today in quietness, and in confidence, you have found rest.

The false obligations and responses due to unmerited guilt will not be able to move you anymore. Because Love

Himself is now carrying you, you can only go where He is going. Activity born from this place of rest in His arms will come, and is what will count for eternity.

Sincere desire does produce action, but for now the sincerity of your heart has brought you rest that will last.

Enjoy the stillness of increasing anticipation that continues to move in your heart.

Going across the threshold of His love, you will find yourself placed much deeper into His heart than when He first picked you up. Here you will discover what is really hidden in your heart. You will discern clearly between the good, and the bad, and then will be able to determine what should remain.

There is such a thin line between judgment and discernment, and as you judge yourself rightly, you will have true discernment.

There is no condemnation in love.

There is something bigger going on...and so much more than meets the eye.

As you take the audit of your heart, you will see things you never realized were inside.

Do not despair; you will also discover a wealth of love now transforming even what you knew to be there for many years. A divine realigning is taking place within, and will affect all of your relationships and activities from now on.

You now understand that how you invest your affections and time really does matter in light of eternity. It is almost like you are having a heart transplant. As He carries you, perhaps at times you will feel like you have been placed into an isolation unit. Sometimes, for your own sake, He must pull you away. You will not be hidden in His arms forever, but for now it is the safest place. What is happening inside you is critical; it will impact the rest of your life...and eternity as well.

He is guarding over you jealously!

Perhaps before others could 'make' you do things you did not really want to do. That should never happen again. The first time you say "No" it will be hard. People will be shocked, and perhaps not even believe you. But you know this new resolution inside is strengthening you with might, and is way beyond anything you could have worked up on your own.

Suddenly you have become aware of His presence more and more, and His pleasure as well.

Nothing else seems to matter, or rather everything else matters like never before.

No one will be able to change your mind once you know His will. You now make decisions out of the desire for His desire that pulses within you. Man will not be able to manipulate you, even if it seems like a golden opportunity they come to offer. You are learning to hear His Voice. Knowing His heart involves more than just being able to hear "Yes" or "No" about the decisions you are facing.

The inner knowing speaks loud and clear.

You have developed such a hunger for His Will.

There is a trembling that comes as you consider your scheduled activities. You understand, that where you are, and who you are with, and what you are doing, all have eternal impact. To a depth and degree you never knew existed before, you long not just know and desire His will, but to be quick in following it.

Delayed obedience is disobedience. Moment by moment the desire for His desire overrides your own. When you are unclear as to what your response needs to be, as you ask for His desire, it will become clear. Those things that use to appeal to your heart and fill you with uncertainty, will no longer find any empty space. You are filled with His love, and now only the things that are born of love can fit within you.

You want all your days to count for eternity sake.

You are gaining a heart of wisdom and revelation for everything in life that will come. Never again will you be taken away from Him. You must remain in His Presence. It is the only place you can breath any more. God is fine-tuning the relationships that touch your life, and setting boundaries you could never have marked out on your own. Your heart is being expanded in the process.

And yes, you are becoming like Him after all!

You want your heart to be without offense when He comes on that great and terrible day. He is an all-consuming fire. Being aware of His Presence every day will cause you to live for the day when you will see Him face to face. Eternal perspective is granted by living each day as if it were that one. A heart of wisdom causes you to make each day count.

Communion with Him, remembering His death as He instructed in the gospels, will cause you to live like never before.

This is the day.

If you knew this was to be the last day you were going to be on earth, your thoughts and actions and words would all be different. They would resound with an eternal perspective that would cover everything, and everyone, with the same love that has been lavished on you. You have been forgiven.

Your slate has been wiped clean.

Forgiveness is a gift, not just to be received, but shared with everyone around you.

The One who forgives us all, long before we ask, will eventually touch even those who refuse your offer of mercy right away. Love really covers a multitude of sins. Love does not expose sin. Love covers over sin by the blood shed on the cross. With acts of kindness and mercy towards others, your own heart is cleansed and begins to resound like His.

You could never become so heavenly minded that you are no earthly good. The only good you will leave on this earth is what springs from a perspective far beyond what can be seen. Eyes of love see beyond every sin, and look to the Savior. Mercy helps others to see Him as they look into your eyes.

Look beyond your own sin and that of others around you. Keep your eyes on the One who showed you the truth, the reality, that mercy triumphs over judgment.

Every time, love wins.

You have been set free from guilt and condemnation.

You know the truth.

You are free indeed.

As you respond to His love, your heart continues to grow in the freedom only love can offer. Finally you are delivered from yourself. Vain imaginations and illusions and delusions all find their power has been broken. There have been too many times when you were your own worse enemy. You did not know that He loved you. There was nothing anyone else could say to you that could affect you more than your own view of who you thought you were, but not any more, and never again.

You now look past what is visible to the cross.

You now live your life in daily communion with Him.

Because you have given Him your heart, the perspective you have of yourself has changed. This might be making you feel a little awkward. You know you are not supposed to hate yourself, but loving yourself seems just a little too foreign.

You do not want to be full of pride. You know pride is a sin. Well, so is false humility! Truth is truth, and the truth is you are loved. Jesus loves you with the same love that the Father loves Him. Now it is His love resounding within you, and for you. The exchange that occurs is real, and will never cease to flow.

You have given Him your heart, and He is giving you His.

A holy and divine exchange is occurring.

You now bear His heart, which can never grow cold.

Your thoughts are being changed by His which will never lead you astray. Your view of life is being broadened by His which is eternal. You knew God was on the move, and leaped up when He reached out His arms to pick you up. Now it is you on the move in His arms.

The suddenly of God is upon you.

All the years of waiting have been swallowed up, in this very moment.

Things seem to be going at an accelerated rate now.

You hang on just a little tighter, and are peering forward with expectancy.

Perhaps others you watched, who just passed you by, seemed like they were really going somewhere. Finally He came close, and stopped right in front of you. Now you are moving with purpose and clear direction. You can only see a little bit in front of you when you look, but He is steady in every step He takes.

Right now you are enjoying being held close enough to look into His eyes.

His confidence in love is empowering you with love.

You are becoming one with Him at last. All of His riches in glory are yours.

You are even beginning to experience some of them as your own; the triumph of mercy over judgment; the victory of love over hatred; healing for your soul and body as well; courage and confidence. Joy that is unspeakable resounds within you.

There is a scene in the gospel of Matthew when Jesus was on His way to heal a local official's daughter. A woman comes up and touches the hem of the garment He was wearing. She was confident that if she could just touch His garment, she would be healed. She had been sick for a long time. She did not want Him to stop for her, just to heal her. She had spent all of her savings on this illness, and suffered much in the hands of others who were attempting to help her.

The situation was beyond desperate. A bold determination pressed her beyond what was acceptable in those days. Things had to change. She could not go on living in that condition. She did not want to. You know the feeling. Something had to happen.

There is a stepping outside of the lines of that which is considered normal, of that is considered respectable, that propels those who recognize Him as He is, to reach out as well.

As she stretched out her hand, and touched the hem of His garment, the healing virtue within Him flowed out freely.

She was made well immediately!

She could not escape being noticed by Jesus now, for He suddenly stopped moving and was looking all around. He asked the crowd that was pressing in so close who had just 'touched' Him. Then Jesus set His eyes upon her, and she came forward.

He called her by name, a name she never expected to hear. He called her, "Daughter". The next sentence says, "the woman" was healed from that moment. The daughter became a woman when she stepped forward. Soon you will be taking a few steps of your own.

You are now closer to Him than she was. You are held in His arms. You are clinging as He carries you across the threshold. At the same time, you can feel Him moving through the corridors of your heart. Now you see more than ever before, that your life is not just hidden, but fully alive, in the chambers of His heart.

The becoming one is really happening.

Resting in His arms you are walking like never before.

Tears were the precious seed that softened your heart.

When you came to the end of your own strength, you were empowered by His love.

You cried out, to get out, out of the valley of the shadow of death. He is the way, the truth, and the life. Not only have you been picked up in the safety of His arms, but also you have been moving by the power of His love.

You have found the place you want to be for the rest of your life, with Him.

You were praying long before you ever picked up this book.

CHAPTER THREE

- His arms are opened now as when you first met

- You have been set in place

- You are standing in the place of authority called prayer

- In His presence there is fullness of joy

- From this place you can go anywhere

- You have been commissioned by sight

- His yoke is easy and His burden so light

- As you open your mouth, He is filling it

- You remember He is good

- His word is alive and active, and now you are as well

- You are no longer content to rest in love

- You will go out and proclaim His love

- All things are possible with Him

- He is generous and extravagant

- Jesus is praying for you right now

- Your life is hidden in Him

- He is alive in you

- Now you carry Him as He carried you

- Together you go out into the world that is waiting

- You are walking in righteousness

- A holy resolution is propelling you forward

- You are growing in the knowledge of God

- You are filled with joy and peace in believing

- He will establish you in love

- His gaze of love has opened your eyes to see

- God's "Kingdom" has come...in you

- His peace is so invigorating

- You are a living stone

- You are a worshipper

- Faith with power is moving you forward

- You are part of His blueprint from heaven for today

- The joy of the Lord is your strength

- He is expressing Himself now through you

- You want to be where He is, so you will go out

- Tradition has its place, and so do you

- He needs no defense

- Every eye will see Him

- There are modern day martyrs all around

- You do make a difference

- Pray for the peace of Jerusalem

There is a subtle stillness all around.
You begin to snuggle in closer.
You are so comfortable in His arms.
There is a silence now that can be heard.
Suddenly, you realize He has stopped moving. You begin to feel Him gently lower you to the ground. He releases you slowly. You are now standing on your own. You feel a little bit taller than when He first picked you up.
You begin to stretch all around.
You have been set in place.
You turn around and see the smile on His face. His arms are opened now just as they were when you first met Him. You can see a different sparkle in His eyes today. You begin to wonder what is happening. He is still close by, and looking in your direction, yet just beyond you at the same time. He puts His hands gently on your shoulders. There is a longing in Him that makes you turn to look and see what has caught His attention.
You are now standing side by side.
There is a vast sea of humanity right before you.
He slowly lifts His hands and stretches them as far as they can go.
He then begins to move forward.
You are standing still confident in love.
It seems that from this place you can go anywhere.

He is ready to be on the move again, and if you want to go with Him, you must take a few steps on your own. He has invited you to go with Him. This is as exciting as when you were first picked up in His arms. You have to respond. He wants you to be with Him where He is. You must respond without delay. Now you know that you belong to Him, that you belong with Him where He is, and wherever He goes.

As always, the choice is yours.

Before, you needed Him to carry you, but not now.

You have been refreshed and refurbished.

You are able to move on your own.

You are confident in love.

You know that He will never leave you. This is His promise, and you know He cannot lie. You realize also that you alone determine whether or not you will go forward with Him. Such passion is rising inside of you that you cannot stand still for very long. It is easy to catch up to Him.

A spark of concern for humanity within you now causes your eyes to shine like His.

You are beginning to realize that this life with Him is not going to be as predictable as it was when you would try to plan for yourself. Because He makes all things new, change is the only constant you will be familiar with from now on. You have poured out your love and devotion as a drink offering to Him, and now your life is going to become like living waters for a thirsty world.

This life of prayer is really a romance about all of mankind.

You remember you really are living life for just one day.

The day when you will see Him face to face, for real, forever, is what really matters to you. What you do with this day is going to affect that day, and you are very aware of this fact. It is not fear that motivates you any longer; it is love and love alone.

Love is the first and great commandment.

God is love, and because of love, you must respond to this new invitation.

It is easier than you thought it would be. Before He picked you up and carried you, "Yes" never came easy at all. Whenever anything involved taking you out of your comfort zone, "No" was a simple answer.

He is your comfort now, and you want to be wherever He is.

You have come to realize this quest to learn to pray has caused you to become a worshipper, not just one who can say prayers. The love in your heart wells up in thanksgiving and praise every time you begin to tell Him how much you love Him.

A joy unspeakable fills your heart each time you look in His direction.

In His presence there is fullness of joy.

As you worship, suddenly you become even more aware of His nearness, and no request seems beyond your hearts desire. He is the answer to your prayers. Conversations with Him are filled with so much love that they lead you to speak together of others He carries in His heart. The circumstances of your own life, which used to be so overwhelming, have now taken their proper perspective.

Concern for others now occupies your heart, just like His. The weight of your own world is finally swept away as tender waves of His love wash over you. The rhythm of His heart sways within you like never before, and the horizon beckons you forward. He is somehow closer now than when you were held in His arms.

You know all things are possible with Him.

A holy resolution in your soul is propelling you forward.

You are now standing in the place of authority called intersession.

This resolution within is birthing a holy revolution all around you.

The reality of partnering with Him has caused you to grow in faith.

You want to see His Kingdom come on earth. You must see His Kingdom come, in reality. You long for others to know Him as you are beginning to. He who walks on water, runs with the clouds, and paints the sky, has invited you to go out into the world He made, with Him.

You will be able to touch those who have not yet responded to His invitation of love.

You have been commissioned by sight.

Your sight is fixed on Him.

Now you can say to the weary one that He will come to them, and save them, as He has saved you. Your life is evidence to a lost and empty world that Jesus is alive. You labored to learn to pray, and found yourself now resting in love with the One who is the answer to all prayer.

This rest is really so invigorating, and fascinating, that you simply walk with ease.

You have entered into His rest because you have ceased from your own striving.

Today you can go out with joy because He is with you.

His yoke is easy, and His burden is light.

You stand as His ambassador.

You represent Him, and His "Kingdom" of Love, everywhere you go. You are a light bearer, and a life giver. Your voice is full of confidence, and love. He has loved you so well.

As you open your mouth, He is filling it.

His voice can be heard in yours.

You now know that God is good, and proclaim it unashamedly, and are unconvinced of any evidence daring to state otherwise. No matter what you see or feel, the reality of His love and goodness sweeps away the looming clouds of darkness and doubt. "God is good" will never just be a saying to you ever again. It is the truth that led you to believe in His love personally. It has become your own reality ever since you were picked up in His arms and carried across the threshold.

You have now been set firmly in place, in love, because of His goodness.

You have been invited into the mystery called "a life of prayer".

From this place, vision is granted, beyond what is visible.

You can hear what no man has any words to speak.

A holy wonder prevails.

You can hear His Voice of love resounding within your heart, and so will everyone around you. Some who have never heard of His goodness, and had life declare boldly to them that He is not good, will soon believe and trust in His love, as you do.

You will carry His goodness and mercy to all who will listen…and to a few who might not listen right away!

Even as He brings judgment to the world, it is an act of His love.

If that statement takes you by surprise, choose to refocus your heart on Him again. Do not be distracted. Every detail of the things He wants you to know will fall into place with time. As you seek Him, as you study the Bible, as those who teach the word with accuracy inspire you, the answers you desire will become yours to pass on to those around you.

The passion of His love has awakened your heart. Now you do not want to see anyone perish either. You will go and tell of His love so none will be caught unaware. This journey of loving Him more and more will pave the way before you. His passion for you, will grant a passion within, which will take you by surprise.

You will have a new hunger to hear Him speaking to you all the time.

The Bible will now be read as His love letter to you.

Because you know you are truly His beloved, it will speak to you in a very personal way. You will hear His voice unfolding mysteries that seemed so impossible to grasp the last time you looked.

His word is alive and active, and now you are too.

No longer will you be content to rest in His love, you must proclaim it.

You do not need to be carried any longer, not right now.

There is now great grace to take a step forward.

You are growing up in love.

You are becoming mature in love.

You can walk on your own because you want to walk in His ways. You are now a messenger of the uncontainable One. You are so full of His love that you must pass it on to others.

Faith with power is beginning to move you forward.

You understand the wisdom of love when it had to constrain you, and yet now you realize the propelling force that love has is much stronger. How you spend your time, money, and affections, demonstrates the condition of your heart. The Author of love has conditioned your heart to beat like His does, and every area of your life is being affected as well.

He is a generous and extravagant giver.

You will now become radical in these areas as well.

The more you learn about Him, the more you will see yourself acting like He does.

Suddenly you realize this lifestyle is a message of hope and truth not just for you, but the whole world as well. When you begin sharing the reality of this love with those around you, some will even join with you in this journey of prayer.

Prayer that is effective goes far beyond mere words that even the best orator can articulate.

Your life speaks clearer than any words, and crosses over every cultural barrier.

Your life of serving God is not just accomplished in your private place of devotion.

You will go and serve others now through charitable deeds and acts of kindness that flow out of your heart of love.

A life of prayer begins in the secret place, but it does not remain in there.

All of your time and resources will be involved in pouring out your life. Choosing to embrace fasting and forgiveness will enable you to do this with a pure heart.

True forgiveness is demonstrated, not only in words, but also through actually blessing your adversaries when you are able. Embracing this lifestyle is essential in living the life of prayer that helps you grow in love.

Remember, the meek really do inherit the earth, even today.

Jesus says in the gospel of Matthew that He came to serve. Now you have come into this life of prayer, to go out, and serve as well. Giving of your time, resources, affections, and strength, are all evidence of a heart of love, and a life of prayer. You can give your time by meeting the practical needs of others through the skills and talents that have been developed over the years. You will still give of your resources by tithing, and even practical and extravagant gifts now beyond that, to help others who are highlighted within your heart.

You pour out your affections by praying and caring for those others tend to forget.

Jesus loves the widow, the orphan, and the poor. He wants you to as well.

You give of your strength every time you fast. Fasting seems at first like you are doing nothing at all, but feeling hunger pains! However, this powerful form of prayer has nothing to do with starving in the natural. When you go without physical nourishment, the scriptures really become alive to you. As you go without food, the word becomes your daily bread, in a more literal sense than normal. A true physical weakness will occur, but might rises up in your inner man, and you are spiritually much more alert and active.

Fasting is not a means to gain approval or persuade the heart of God, it tenderizes and moves our own heart to beat like His. Jesus said that some prayers are only answered when strengthened with fasting. Unbelief is uprooted and another measure of faith is added to yours when a fasting lifestyle is embraced.

Fasting is so powerful and effective that Jesus did it, and encourages you to as well.

True meekness, when motivated from a heart of love that longs for His glory, will avail much. As you take hold of Him in the secret place, you will begin to live a lifestyle that confounds every evil force, and all of mankind as well. Yours will not be the only life that is changed. There is a place for human effort, but it is not necessary in the area of prayer. In prayer, you simply spend your time and your affection, by bringing to God that which is beyond your ability to meet without His intervention.

Forgiveness is a wonderful example.

Forgiveness is a choice.

Yes, you can forgive, and now you know that you must.

Forgiveness is choosing to deliberately extend a blessing to others in the place of prayer. Then you will be inspired to secretly begin doing acts of kindness from a heart of love, which will set the captive free. Praying for anyone who has harmed you, in any way, will keep your own heart clean. You cannot hold an offense towards someone you take time to ask God to bless and heal and love.

The merciful shall be shown mercy.

You are called to lay down your life, in love.
Then you will be standing like never before.
Love your enemies and do good to those who have not been good to you.
Your life will be making a way for others to come to Christ. Then they can walk into the freedom of forgiveness as well. You will not just be confident in God's love for yourself, but you will see His heart of love for others around you.
Abide in the mercy of God's heart, and from there you will be able to forgive anyone, in love. The truth that has set you free is the only way to true freedom for anyone on earth. Forgiveness is not foolishness, but often appears as such to the world.
God came to set the captives free.
The truth is, mercy will always triumph over judgment, even the judgment in your own heart. The freedom your heart longs for must not be delayed a moment longer. You need to keep your heart clean and tender before Him. Too many around you are perishing for lack of knowledge…the knowledge of His love and mercy.
Forgiving is the wisest thing you will ever do.
He is waiting for them, like He waited for you.
You must not wait any longer.
Life is hard, and man is not good, but God is good.
Let your tears flow like a healing river, and forgive now.
He reveals Himself as good all through the Bible.
Truth sets everyone free. Truth is a Man, and His name is Jesus. That sounds a little strange at first, but you might come to say "Truth is a Man" yourself one day as the love of the truth renews your mind. He allured you even in the wilderness seasons of your life, and has brought you forth with joy for this day.
God is faithful, and full of mercy and love and joy.
He knew you would say, "Yes" to Him. Every day He rejoiced over your life, confidently in love. Remember He is

the Great Intercessor. He gets every prayer answered. Your life is an answer to the prayer of His heart.

Even now He is at the right hand of the Father interceding for you.

As you come to know Him more, and because you come to believe the view He has of you, you will be able to bear His heart for the world around you. You are His ambassador in this life of prayer. The Spirit of Grace and Supplication is the true essence of prayer. It is by grace you were saved, and by grace that you will be sustained in this life of prayer, even if with deep groaning at times.

He will give you the right prayers to pray as you listen to His heart.

He does what only He can do, with delight.

Your life is hidden in Him and He is alive within you.

Now, you carry Him as He carried you, and together you go out into the world.

Christ in you is the hope of glory.

The Bible tells us that the knowledge of the glory of the Lord will cover the earth as the waters cover the sea. Today He covers the earth embodied in the lives of those who love Him.

He lives in you.

You are now standing in love, and love of the truth.

You have been taken out of religion and delivered into reality.

You are walking in righteousness and increasing in the knowledge of God.

Being joyful in Him takes you from being one who prays, to one who praises.

He trains your hands for war and fingers for the battle in the place of worship.

Can you play a musical instrument, play now for His glory.

Can you clap your hands, loudly applaud His love. Can you comfort someone in sorrow, go and do so today. You will be going from strength to strength, and from glory to glory, when you dwell in the secret place of prayer. Then, as your mind is renewed, you will begin to make prophetic declarations that spring from the scriptures you are mediating on each day.

These will be the prayers that will impact many lives besides your own.

Those who know their God will be strong and do exploits.

You will be strengthened with might in your inner man as Christ dwells in your heart. You will begin to walk in wisdom and revelation that is supernatural, and it will become natural for you to ask! You will be fruitful in every good work and increase in the knowledge of God day by day as you pray His word back to Him.

God Himself will fill you with all joy and peace in believing.

Now you will abound in hope that does not disappoint, and pass it on to all around you. This happens when you are rooted and grounded in love. As He was carrying you across the threshold, deep roots of love were nurtured and strengthened, just by His nearness.

Your roots are growing deeper every day in His love.

You were, and are even now, enriched in everything, in Him.

He is establishing you in His Love.

There is a communion revival beginning to stir across the face of the earth.

The longing for His presence is birthing a deeper passion than the church has ever walked in before. As those who are His own begin to remember and proclaim His death, many will come to life.

Jesus was made manifest in the flesh to destroy the works of the devil.

Now, where you go the Kingdom of God will prevail.

As you ask and seek and knock, you will not be deigned, neither will those you make petitions for. Intercession is putting Jesus in remembrance of what He has declared in the Bible. As you do this, you will begin to embrace all that Christ has for you. We all are given a measure of faith, but you can always ask the One who loves to give, for more!

The steady gaze of His love for you has opened your eyes to see like never before.

All the things you see now, He has been looking at with love, and waiting for you to look at from His perspective of love as well. He gives you vision and direction on to how to pray.

God's kingdom has come…in you! He opens His hand to satisfy the desire of all things.

Your desire for Him has caused your hands to now become as opened as His are.

You will serve others with joy, all for love, with the love that never fails.

There is a steadiness now in your steps, like you felt in His. He is with you and has assigned angels to guard you along the way even when you cannot feel His presence.

You are the scepter in His hand so others can get close to Him.

He holds you out, to draw them in.

You are held safe in every step.

The welcome that others can feel in your words is really an invitation from His heart.

The conversations of the godly are recorded in a book of remembrance. You might not even be aware of the encouragement you speak, but not one word goes unnoticed by the Author of such love. He fills your heart so full that you just have to open your mouth. Many lives around you are hungry and thirsty. They will draw Him out of you without you even realizing what is going on.

You do not have to premeditate love; it will just flow out naturally from your heart.

You need to be fed daily from the word yourself, and as you do, there will be enough of a supply, that those around you will be filled as well. When you begin to pray the scriptures back to Him, you will find they come out in all your conversations with others. You are a different person now, and so is your speech. You are so aware of the holy acceleration that has begun, and you want others to understand this time in history is like no other.

You have come out of your comfort zone.

You have seen Jesus in a new way, and yourself as well.

You gladly embrace the changes that love has brought your way.

You have come to realize that church, as you know it, is changing also. It had to.

There is a new church emerging.

It is a church without walls, which is being administered by the Holy Spirit. Remember this book is not about doctrine, new or old, it is about the reality of a life of prayer. The true church is made up of living stones,

Buildings are necessary, and tradition has its place, but you have discovered in these pages that you have one as well.

True life is found beyond the structures that have been fashioned by man.

Human lives must be built, built together. You will follow the Lamb, anywhere. No fear or compromise or opinion will hold you back ever again. This world holds nothing for you, except the opportunity of introducing others to the soon returning Lion of Judah.

He is the Lamb and the Lion indeed!

Now you are a worshiper, a worshiping warrior, because you live a life of prayer.

Many pray who do not know Him. You remember that you had at one time. Since you have become a worshipper, you have begun to pray with a confidence and a boldness never known before. The delight and anticipation over each answer grows as you gain His heart and perspective for the world beyond your own limited view.

You are part of the blue print from heaven for these last days.

You are part of this chosen generation...no matter what age you are.

You are not too old, or too young, to begin this life of prayer.

You were made to walk where the streets are paved with gold and to live where your treasure cannot be stolen...but for now there is concrete and gravel and dirt to be tread upon.

You will walk in love.

Imagine yourself as a bride walking down the isle. Each day, each step, carries you closer to the destiny you were created for, which is standing by His side. As you become more and more aware of His gaze of love upon you, and His longing for you to be by His side, the radiance of a Bride will adorn you. This book is not about gender either. Remember guys, women are called the sons of God, and so you can be known as the bride of Christ.

We are all complete in Him without any confusion!

His gaze of love upon you will not leave Him waiting at the altar for you to arrive on your own. Even now as you read, He is taking steps closer towards that day when you will be by His side forever.

Remember the picture of how He longs for you. As you look for that day, you are hastening His return. He will not delay much longer. He does what only He can do, and wants you do what you were created to do, simply be with Him. As you partner with Him to see His Kingdom come on earth, suddenly, every eye will see Him. Not everyone thinks they are an intercessor, and even fewer desire such a thing to be true. But now this is your passion.

You have seen that learning to pray is not about doing something, it is about becoming the one you were created to be, His partner on the earth. Most have no knowledge of what that really means, but you have now been given a glimpse. Because you have become one with the Great Intercessor, and since you are made in His image, you will be an intercessor for all of eternity. You have already begun doing this.

It is like you have slipped into this shoreless ocean of His love as you go about your daily life of prayer. He is seeing through the lattice of the atmosphere, gazing through the window of time, to watch you. As you become aware of His steady gaze, you will walk worthy.

There is no fear in this life of love, and you go forth with joy.

Your life is His answer to the heart cry of the world.

Each step you take will have purpose and value.

You will now live every day to the full.

The joy of the Lord is your strength.

So many do not yet believe in Him, but you do, and now many others will. A stream of living water flows out of you from deep within...alive with love.

God is the river of life and this life is moving you every step along the way. You are a living report of all that is eternally true. As people see you, they will see Him.

You are the only Bible some people will ever read.

There is something more than just your personal love story being birthed as you pray. You have aligned your heart with His so others will see Him, and come to love Him as well.

He is expressing Himself now in you!

You want to be with Him where He is...so you must go into the world.

As you begin to ask the Father for the release of His Son, you realize so many on earth need to be set free before He can come. His delay is full of mercy so others can be with Him forever, just like you will be. You will run the race set before you and help others to run as well.

He is your great reward in this life.

You have been taken out of religion and delivered into reality.

You are standing in the reality of His love, and now walk in righteousness.

Daily you are increasing in the knowledge of God, and want others to know Him too. You are one of the voluntary lovers who show the way to Him is through love and not argument.

He needs no defense.

His peace now propels you.

He is able to show His love to any who will look for it.

Those who know their God will be strong and do exploits.

As the pieces of your life are put back together, peace is restored, in you.

Whenever a revival has occurred, it was through the blood of those who proclaimed the reality of His precious blood. The blood of those whose lives are taken by those who ignore and despise the cross, also declare it. Modern day martyrs are dying in our land as abortion is claiming the lives of the innocent. It is like in the days of Moses and Jesus when laws were put in place to destroy a generation full of holy seed.

The day is coming when either you, or your children, will loose their lives as other laws are implemented to silence the voice of truth that dares to proclaim His blood that was shed.

As you embrace His cross, yours will become easier to bear.

Finally, keep your eyes on Israel for they are a special treasure in the heart of God.

Jesus could have come to earth in any tribe or nation, but the Jewish people are His people by choice. When He returns to claim this earth as His own, it will be in a Jewish body.

Every eye will see Him on that day. Let your heart be pierced now and cry out for the peace
of Jerusalem as He is doing.

You have heard His Voice of Love.

Now you understand it is your voice that really, really, does matter, more than ever before. You will begin to proclaim all that is contained here, and never be silenced again! Your life does make a difference.

This is the end of the book, but not the end of your story.

THE STARFISH STORY

Once upon a time there was an old man who used to go to the ocean early in the mornings. He had a habit of walking on the beach for a mile or two before he went to work.

One day he was walking along the shore. As he looked down the beach, he saw a human figure moving like a dancer. He smiled to himself to think of someone who would dance to the day. So he began to walk faster to catch up.

As he got closer, he saw that it was a young man and the young man wasn't dancing, but instead he was reaching down to the shore, picking up something and very gently throwing it into the ocean. As he got closer he called out, "Good morning! What are you doing?"

The young man paused, looked up and replied, "Throwing starfish in the ocean." "I guess I should have asked, 'why are you throwing starfish in the ocean?'" "The sun is up and the tide is going out. And if I don't throw them in they'll die." "But, young man, don't you realize that there are miles and miles of beach and starfish all along it. You can't possibly make a difference!" The young man listened politely. Then bent down picked another starfish and threw it into the sea past the breaking waves and said, "It made a difference for that one".

=-=

The preceding is adapted from The Star Thrower by anthropologist Loren Eiseley (1907-1977). The story has appeared all over the web and been printed in various articles with no credit given to its author. There are variations that use different 'stars' in the beach scene, so today put in your own name as the main character, and do what you know will really make a difference for at least one!

SCRIPTURE REFERENCES

Introduction Scriptures

2 Peter 1:10 Jesus invited you into this life of prayer.

James 1:8 False realities will be dismantled with the truth of His word.

Acts 3:19 Being in His presence is prayer.

Acts 17:18 We are mobile houses of prayer.

Mark 8:34; 1 Corinthians 1:18; Galatians 6:14; Colossians 1:20 Life begins at the cross.

Romans 8:28 All things work together for the good for those who love Him and are called according to His purpose.

John 3:16 Romance is in His blood. Now you can live with Him forever!

Matthew 5:8 We become what we behold.

Psalms 118:24 This is the day.

Acts 20:32 Grace is your inheritance to build you up.

John 14:17 The Spirit of Truth is with you.

Mark 10:16 He has opened arms of love.

John 15:9 He will never grow cold or withdraw His affection towards you.

2 Corinthians 5:17; Revelation 21:5 He really makes all things new, and that means ALL.

Romans 7:22 Delight in the word of God.

1 John 4:19 We love Him, because He first loved us.

Matthew 9:36 He looks through lenses of love alone.

2 Corinthians 3:17 You are free to stand in life, and in love.

Colossians 3:3 Your life is hidden in His.

Chapter One Scriptures

Matthew 22:14 You have been chosen.

John 17:24 He desires you to be with Him.

1 John 4:18 His love removes all fear.

1 Corinthians 4:5 Nothing is hidden from His gaze.

1 Corinthians 12:9; Nehemiah 8:10 God gives you strength. The joy of the Lord is your strength.

Lamentations 3:22-23 His mercy is new every morning.

Psalm 139:13-17 No one knows the real you like He does. He formed and fashioned you individually.

Genesis 1:27 You are made in the image of God.

1 John 4:19 You love Him because He first loved you.

Mark 12:30 You are commanded to love Him first.

John 8:32 Knowing the truth sets you free.

Revelations 21:5 He makes all things new.

John 1:5 Light shines into the darkness.

Isaiah 61:3 He gives you real beauty for ashes.

Psalm 96:9; Psalm 110:3 Holiness beautifies you.

1 Peter 2:5 You are holy to the Lord.

2 Chronicles 16 He is looking at you.

The entire book of Esther You have access to the King of Kings!

John 15:16 God chose you.

Revelations 4:1 You are invited to "Come".

Daniel 2:28, 47 God reveals secrets.

Psalm 147:4 God named every star.

Psalm 139:16 He knew you long before you were born.

Deuteronomy 7:6 You are His favorite, a special treasure.

John 20:11-19 This is the story of Mary seeing Jesus after He rose from the dead.

John 14:3 Jesus is coming again.

Ephesians 4:8; 2 Peter 3:9 He is rich in mercy and does not want anyone to perish.

Acts 14:3 Jesus will confirm His word as you speak it.

Matthew 10:19 He wants to speak to you.

Daniel 2:47 God wants to reveal secrets to you.

Ezekiel 16:8; Song of Solomon 7:10 It is your time for love.

Job 8:21 God fills you with laughter.

Psalm 127:2; Exodus 15:2 He gives you rest. He is your strength.

Nehemiah 8:10; 2 Corinthians 7:4 The joy of the Lord is your strength.

Isaiah 61:7 Instead of shame, you get a double portion of joy.

Song of Solomon 8:5 You are leaning on your Beloved.

Isaiah 59:16; Hebrews 7:25; Romans 8:34 Jesus is praying for you.

2 Timothy 3:4 There are God lovers and God haters being set apart today.

John 17 One of the prayers Jesus prayed for you.

Luke 24:39 Jesus has marks of love in His body forever.

Revelation Chapters 4 and 5 Describing some scenes of worship in heaven.

Colossians 2:10 You are complete in Him.

Matthew 7:7 Seek and you will find.

Ephesians 3:19 When you know the love of Christ, you will be filled with all the fullness of God.

Colossians 3:3 Your life is hidden in Christ. R

Romans 5:5; 15:13 Hoping in Him will not disappoint you.

Romans 12:2 God wants you to know His will.

Psalms 56:8 He has gathered all your tears.

Psalms 46:1 He is a very present help in trouble.

Psalms 94:22 He is your defense.

John 1:14; 2 John 1:7 God came in the flesh and dwelt among us.

Luke 22:44 Jesus sweat great drops of blood in the garden.

Luke 22:63 Jesus bled internally when He was beaten.

Isaiah 53:5 By His stripes, you are healed.

Psalm 103:3 Jesus heals ALL diseases, and forgives ALL sins.

John 19:30 Jesus said, "It is finished".

John 19:37 His side was pierced.

Song of Solomon His body is like carved ivory, inlaid with sapphires.

Josh 3:11; Zech 6:5; Acts 10:36 Jesus is Lord of all.

Song of Solomon 4:16 He sends both the winds of testing and blessing upon your life.

Psalm 86:7; 91:15; Isaiah 65:24; Jeremiah 33:3 Jesus wants to answer you.

My glimpse of the 7 ways Christ bled was gathered by permission from Perfect Redemption by Dr. Dale M. Sides. There are many variations and views, and so I have also intertwined my own in this book.

Chapter Two Scriptures

Isaiah 46:4 He will carry you even in your old age.

Deuteronomy 3:24; 2 Samuel 22:33; Isaiah 35:4 God is strong, and you are safe.

Isaiah 54:10 God has given you a covenant of peace.

Psalm 42:5,11; 42:5; 71:14; Jeremiah 29:11; 31:17; Zechariah 9:12; Rom 5:15; 15:13 You have lots of hope for the future, and will not be disappointed.

Song of Solomon 8:5 This is the description of the bride, coming out of the wilderness and leaning on her beloved.

Colossians 2:8; 1 Corinthians 15:35; James1:16 You are freed from vain imaginations and deception.

Romans 8:28; 1 John 5:2 You are a God lover.

Mark 9:31 You belong to God.

Romans 15:13 You have joy and peace in believing.

John 10:3 You hear His voice.

Isaiah 43:7 You were created for His glory.

Exodus 12 The story of the first Passover is in this chapter.

Luke 22:15 Jesus tells of His fervent desire to eat this Passover meal with His disciples.

1 Corinthians 1:18 Life for you was the purpose of Jesus death on the cross.

Hebrews 12:2 You are the joy set before Him.

Matthew 22:37-40 Love others as you love yourself. This is only possible by loving Him first.

Matthew 5:5 The humble inherit the earth.

Isaiah 5:21; Ephesians 1:17; Colossians 1:9; James 1:5; 3:17 You are not wise in your own opinion. God has granted you wisdom.

Matthew 5:1-12 The Sermon on the Mount describing the character of one who is blessed is found here.

I Corinthians 13 This is the description and value of love that never fails.

Nehemiah 8:10 The joy of the Lord is your strength.

Colossians 2:2 You are to be confident in His love.

Psalm 34:5 You are radiant.

Luke 15:10 The angels rejoiced when you said, "Yes" to Jesus.

Romans 8:28 All things are working together for your good.

Isaiah 64:1-4 God will tear open the heavens and come to you. There is no god like Him who acts in behalf of the one who waits on Him.

Psalms 127:2 He gives you rest.

Song of Solomon 4:16 Winds of adversity and blessing both have carried you into His arms of love.

Psalm 46:10 Be still, and you will know He is God.

Psalm 73:1 God is good.

Hebrews 4:3 You can enter into His rest.

Matthew 25:1-14 Here is the story of the wise and the foolish virgins.

Hebrews 6:18 God cannot lie.

Isaiah 30:15 In quietness and in confidence you have found the strength to rest.

Hebrews 4:12 You can now clearly discern between the thoughts and intentions of your heart.

Galatians 1:15 God has separated you unto Himself.

Deuteronomy 4:24 God is guarding you jealously.

Acts 24:14 God wants you to know His will.

1 Samuel 15:22; 2 Corinthians 10:5; Hebrews 5:8; 1 Peter 1:22; Acts 5:29 Obedience is better than sacrifice, and even Jesus learned obedience.

Ephesians 3:17; Psalm 90:12 You are gaining a heart of wisdom and revelation.

Matthew 6:12-15; 18:21 You are now able to forgive others just as Jesus forgave you.

John 8:32 The truth has set you free.

Philippians 4:19 All His riches in glory are now yours.

Matthew 9:18-26 This is the story of the woman who touched the hem of Jesus' garment.

1 Peter 1:8 You have joy unspeakable and full of glory.

Psalm 126:5 Your tears are precious seed. You shall reap in joy.

Psalm 23:4 He is carrying you out of the valley of the shadow Of death…it is only a shadow!

Chapter Three Scriptures

1 Samuel 12:16; 1 Kings 19:12; 2 Chronicles 20:17; Psalm 4:4; 46:10 Stillness is a good thing.

Joel 3:14 here are so many in the valley of decision needing to know God's love.

Isaiah 55:12; Luke 14:23 You are invited to go out with Him.

Titus 1:2 God cannot lie.

Acts 3:19 You will be refreshed in the presence of the Lord.

Revelation 21:5 He makes all things new.

Song of Solomon 4:15 Living waters are inside of you.

Joel 2:31; Jude 1:6 There is a great and terrible day coming.

Matthew 22:34-40 Love is the first and great commandment.

Psalm 16:11 There is fullness of joy in the presence of the Lord.

Matthew 19:26; Mark 9:23; Mark 10:27 All things are possible.

Matthew 9:8; 10:1; Luke 10:19 You have authority in prayer.

Matthew 2:28; 6:10; Luke 10:9; 11:20 You will see His Kingdom come!

Acts 22:14-15; Matthew 5:8; Luke 3:6; 8:10 You have been appointed to see Jesus and go tell others.

Isaiah 35:4 God will come and save.

Hebrews 4:3 You can enter into His rest.

Matthew 11:29 His burden is light.

Psalm 81:10 When you open your mouth, God will fill it.

Psalm 9:7-8; 76:9; Zechariah 7:9; 8:16 God brings judgment into the world as an act of love for those who love Him.

Hebrews 4:12 The scriptures are alive and active...in you!

2 Corinthians 3:12 Hope gives you great boldness in your speech.

Ephesians 3:15 We grow up when we speak the truth in love.

1 Corinthians 2:5; 2 Thessalonians 1:11 There is faith with power available to you.

Psalm 40:5 God is generous and extravagant.

Matthew Chapters 4-7 The Sermon on the Mount. Giving of yourself in secret is a form of prayer. It is true warfare that is not of this world.

Matthew 17:21; Mark 9:29 Some prayers are only answered when accompanied by fasting.

Matthew 4:6-18 Life in secret will bear much fruit and be rewarded by God.

Jeremiah 31:2; Hosea 2:14 God kept and spoke to you in the wilderness seasons.

Acts 2:33 Jesus is at the right hand of the Father praying for you today.

Zechariah 12:10 The Spirit of Grace and Supplication is the true Spirit of Prayer.

Ephesians 2:8 You were saved by grace. **Colossians 3:3** Your life is hidden in His.

Colossians 1:27 Christ in you is the hope of glory.

2 Thessalonians 2:10; 2 John 3:18 You love the truth.

Philippians 1:9 You are increasing in knowledge.

Psalm 144:1 He trains your hand for war and your fingers for the battle...in worship!

Daniel 11:32 Those who know their God will be strong.

Ephesians 3:16 He is strengthening you with might deep inside.

Ephesians 1:17 He gives wisdom and revelation to you.

2 Thessalonians 2:17 You will be fruitful in every good work.

Romans 15:13 There is peace and joy in believing so you can Abound in hope.

1 John 3:8 Jesus came in the flesh to destroy the works of the devil.

Matthew 7:7 Ask, and you will receive. Seek, and you will find. Knock, and the door will open. Keep on asking, seeking, and knocking...do not give up!

Isaiah 58:11; Psalm 145:19 He will satisfy your desire.

Acts 26:18; Psalm 119:18; Isaiah 42:7; Acts 2:17 He gives you vision.

Psalm 91:11 He has sent angels to guard you.

Malachi 3:16 There is a book of remembrance written Containing your conversations.

1 Peter 2:5 You are a living stone. The church is built from living stones.

Ephesians 2:10 You were created for good works.

John 1:29; Revelation 5:12 Jesus is the Lamb that we slain.

Revelation 5:5; 22:20 Jesus is the soon returning Lion of Judah.

1 Chronicles 16:29; Psalm 29:2; 96:9 Worship the Lord in the beauty of holiness.

1 Peter 2:9 You are part of a chosen generation.

Revelation 21:21 You will walk on streets of gold in heaven.

Matthew 5:9; Romans 8:9; 9:26 You are called a son of God.

Revelation 21:9 You are the Bride of Christ.

Genesis 1:27 God created each of us male or female.

2 Peter 3:11-13 Jesus is not slow about the day of His return. He is not willing for anyone to perish. Because you know this is true you will look for and hasten the day of His return by the way you live your life.

1 John 4:18 There is no fear in love.

Revelation 1:7 Every eye will see Him on the day He returns.

1 Corinthians 9:24; Hebrews 12:1 Run the race set before you, and win.

Genesis 15:1 Jesus is your very great reward.

Exodus 1:22; Matthew 2:16-18 The innocent slaughtered in the days of Moses and Jesus.

Deuteronomy 7:6-9; Psalm 147:2-14 The Jewish people are special to the Lord.

Psalm 122:6 Pray for the peace of Jerusalem.

A FEW NAMES OF GOD

ALPHA AND OMEGA (REVELATION 22:13) He is the beginning and the end of all things.

ALMIGHTY GOD (GENESIS 17:1) He is in control.

AUTHOR OF SALVATION (HEBREWS 5:9) He saved me. He can save anyone!

MY **BELOVED** (SONG OF SOLOMON 2:16) He is mine, and I am His.

MY **CREATOR** (ISAIAH 44:2) He created me, and is able to recreate every cell anew.

CREATOR OF ALL THINGS (COLOSSIANS 1:16) He made me, and everything around me.

COMFORT (ISAIAH 40:1) He knows how to heal my wounds so I will not have any offense.

COUNSELOR (ISAIAH 40:13) He is so wise and will give me wisdom for every decision.

DELIVERER (2 Samuel 22:2) He is the defense of my life.

EMMANUEL, GOD WITH US (MATTHEW 1:23) I am never alone.

FATHER (MATTHEW 5:45) I am His child.

GOD OF ALL PEOPLE (JEREMIAH 32:17) He loves everyone.

GOD WHO FORGIVES (ISAIAH 43:12) He is merciful. He is not mad at me.

GOD WHO SPEAKS (ISAIAH 48:15) He wants me to know His will.

GOOD SHEPHERD (JOHN 10:11) He will not lead me astray.

GREAT REWARD (Genesis 15:1) He is my prize in life.

HEAD OF THE CHURCH (COLOSSIANS 1: 18) He is the final authority.

HEALER (EXODUS 15:26) He wants me to be healthy.

HELPER OF THE NEEDY (HEBREWS 13:6) He likes to meet my needs.

HOPE THAT DOES NOT DISAPPOINT (ROMANS5:5) I believe what He has spoken.

HUSBAND (ISAIAH 54:5) He will protect and keep and love me forever.

JEALOUS (EXODUS 34:14) He will not let anyone come between us.

KEEPER OF ISRAEL (PSALM 121:3-5) He is guarding Israel.

KING OF THE JEWS (MATTHEW 2:2) He especially loves the Jewish people.

KING OF KINGS (REVELATION 19:12) No one has more authority than He does.

LORD OF THE HARVEST (MATTHEW 9:38) He is the author of revival.

LIVING GOD (1 TIMOTHY 4:10) He is alive.

THE ONLY GOD (ISAIAH 45:6, 22) There is no other god.

MASTER OF THE BREAKTHROUGH (1Chronicles14:11; 2 Samuel 5:20; Isaiah 28:21) I will not give up!

OVERCOMER (REVELATION 3:21) He wins every time.

OMNIPRESENT ONE (PSALM 139:4-12) He is everywhere...all the time!

PROTECTOR (ISAIAH 44:6) I am safe.

PROVIDER (GENESIS 22:8) God sees ahead and makes provision for me along the way.

PHYSICIAN (JEREMIAH 8:22) God created me, and is able to keep me healthy.

REDEEMER (ISAIAH 49:6) He has purchased me. I belong to Him.

RESTORER (RUTH 4:14-15) He gets things back to the original design and purpose.

RESURRECTION (JOHN 11:25) He brings dead things to life again.

REVEALER OF SECRETS (ISAIAH 45:3) Nothing is hidden from Him.

REWARDER (RUTH 2:12) He keeps accurate records.

SAVIOR (ISAIAH 44:22) He saved me, and saves me daily.

SON OF MAN (LUKE 19:10) He became flesh and blood just like me.

SON OF GOD (MATTHEW 4:3,6) He is holy divine, wholly other than, Begotten, not made.

SOVEREIGN GOD (EZEKIEL 29:16) Nothing escapes His notice.

SHIELD (GENESIS 15:1) He surrounds me.

STRENGTH (ISAIAH 51:12) He is stronger than any one or anything.

TEACHER (JOHN 3:2; Isaiah 48:17) He knows everything.

TRUTH (DEUTERONOMY 32:4; JOHN 14:6) He has set me free.

UPHOLDER (HEBREWS 1:3) He holds my hand.

VICTOR (PSALM 98: 1) He wins every time.

VINDICATOR (REVELATION 6:9-11) He makes the wrong things right.

WAY TRUTH AND LIFE (JOHN 14:6) He is the ONLY way, to truth and life.

WORD (JOHN 1:1) He is God's communication in every language.

WONDERFUL (Judges 13:18) He even thinks His name is Wonderful!

REFUTING UNGODLY BELIEFS...

S peak outloud what is truth for you personally, then search the scriptures and make your own list

• The lie that God helps those who help themselves
TRUTH BASED ON MATTHEW 9:36 *JESUS IS MOVED WITH COMPASSION FOR ME WHEN I FEEL HELPLESS. HE WILL COME TO ME WHEN I CANNOT GET TO HIM ON MY OWN. HE WANTS TO HELP ME.*

• The lie that you could become so heavenly minded you would be no earthy good
TRUTH BASED ON JOHN 3:6 *I WANT THAT WHICH MATTERS FOR ETERNITY TO CONSUME MY THOUGHTS AND WORDS AND ACTIONS. AS I SET MY GAZE ON JESUS THE THINGS AROUND ME WILL TAKE THEIR PROPER PLACE IN MY HEART.*

• The lie that God is mad at me
TRUTH BASED ON ZEPHANIAH 3:17 *GOD REJOICES OVER ME WITH JOY. HE IS SINGING JOYFULLY OVER MY LIFE RIGHT NOW.*

• The lie that God wants to punish me
TRUTH BASED ON 1 JOHN 1:9; 2 PETER 3:9 *WHEN I CONFESS MY SIN, GOD FORGIVES ME. HE DOES NOT WANT ME TO PERISH.*

• The lie that I am ugly physically
TRUTH BASED ON PSALM 139:14 *I AM FEARFULLY AND WONDERFULLY MADE.*

*The lie that I lack what is needed in this life
TRUTH BASED ON 2 CORINTHIANS 9:8 *I HAVE EVERYTHING I NEED TO ENJOY LIFE.*

• The lie that I am in an impossible situation
TRUTH BASED ON LUKE 18:27 *NOTHING IS IMPOSSIBLE WITH GOD, AND I AM WITH GOD.*

• The lie that I do not have anything to say
TRUTH BASED ON PROVERBS 31:8-9, 26; PSALM 81:10 *I CAN OPEN MY MOUTH FOR THE SPEECHLESS AND PLEAD THE CAUSE OF THE POOR AND NEEDY. I OPEN MY MOUTH WITH WISDOM AND MY SPEECH IS KIND. WHEN I OPEN MY MOUTH, HE FILLS IT.*

• The lie that I am afraid
TRUTH BASED ON PROVERBS 28:1 *THE RIGHTEOUS ARE BOLD AS A LION.*

• The lie that because of my past I am dirty and disqualified.
TRUTH BASED ON ACTS 10:15; ROMANS 5:1, 9 *I AM CLEAN NOW AND JUSTIFIED BY FAITH IN THE BLOOD OF JESUS.*

• The lie that I have to remain sick.
**TRUTH BASED ON ISAIAH 33:24; MATTHEW
8:1617; 1 PETER 2:24;**
PSALM 103:1-2; ACTS 10:38 *JESUS CAN HEAL ME.*
JESUS WANTS TO HEAL ME. I AM HEALED!

• The lie that I am unable to make up my mind.
**TRUTH BASED ON 1 KINGS 18:21; JAMES 1:8;
2TIMOTHY 1:7; 1 CORINTHIANS 2:16** *I WILL NOT
BE DOUBLE-MINDED, I BELIEVE IN GOD. I HAVE
A SOUND MIND. I CAN THINK CLEARLY. I HAVE
BEEN GIVEN THE MIND OF CHRIST.*

• The lie that I won't receive the promise I am hoping for.
**TRUTH BASED ON HEBREWS 10:23, 35;
HEBREWS11:1, 6** *HE WHO PROMISED
IS FAITHFUL, I WILL CONTINUE TO SEEK HIM
AND NOT GIVE UP.*

• The lie that God cannot, does not, love me.
TRUTH BASED ON JEREMIAH 31:3 *GOD LOVES
ME WITH AN EVERLASTING LOVE.*

The International House of Prayer in Kansas City

The International House of Prayer is a missionary organization based in Kansas City, Missouri, that we refer to as the "Missions Base." It is touching thousands of young adults around the world, as well as reaching out to the poor and needy to communicate the healing power and love of Jesus. We currently have a full time staff over 400 people who each raise their financial support to live here as a missionary.

Let me briefly describe the Missions Base. We have developed many different outreach and training ministries that operate together on our Missions Base. Our most unusual ministry is our prayer ministry which has operated 24 hour a day since September 19, 1999, called the International House of Prayer. What surprises people is that each of the 84 (two-hour) prayer meetings each week is led by a worship team. A fasting team supports each prayer/worship meeting. Therefore, prayer and fasting continue non-stop 365 days a year as foundational for our outreach ministries.

Our outreach ministries include feeding the poor, evangelizing, training young people (our passion is training young adults from Third World countries), Healing Rooms that are open to anyone sick who needs prayer, a children's equipping center, various prophetic ministries, an outreach to Israel, training programs that currently train hundreds of young adults. Currently, our students and interns are from about 15 nations. Classes are conducted in several different languages. One of our highlights is a ministry called the Joseph Company that trains and finances young adults to start new businesses that they will own personally.

Our staff is made up of missionaries of all ages ranging from 18- 80. Our training and outreach program reach all ages as well. However, the most responsive age group is young adults. Over 15,000 young adults attended the Call/ One Thing Conference with us here in 2002.

Our staff does missionary work in five ways

1. Prayer - in doing the hard work of prayer and fasting for the release of the Harvest locally and in the nations (Matt. 9:37-38). We also provide diligent prayer covering for missionaries currently on the mission field. Night and day prayer with fasting is a primary Scriptural requirement for the release of revival and the Great Commission.

2. Outreach ministry – to the poor, sick and needy locally and abroad.

3. Training – we have extensive programs to train missionaries desiring to be sent to the nations.

4. Short-term mission trips – our team serve other missionary works across the nations.

5. Being sent - personally relocating to other nations as long-term missionaries.

Staff Requirements – Diligent Work

We require that all our full-time staff missionaries commit themselves to 50 hours per week of dedicated service. This includes helping to lead prayer and worship meetings, training others, evangelism, outreach to the poor, serving in the administrative, etc. Our missionaries maintain a rigorous prayer life with regular fasting as they serve the poor, sick and needy in our outreaches.

Visit our site for more information at http://www.IHOP.org

Ministry of Debra-Louise Cossu

I have longed all my life to let people know that they are loved. We can only give away what we possess ourselves. Moving to be a missionary on the field of prayer here in Kansas City has provided many opportunities for that to occur by serving as the Critical/Chronic Care Manager. I also give leadership to the administration of prayers for the requests that come in over the phone, web, our partners, and those who walk into the prayer room.

Teaching an Encountering Christ Within class that sprung out of leading and training teams in the Bethany Healing room, is one of my greatest joys. As people in pain find peace in the Presence of Christ the healer, healing is made possible in every area.

I am confident in love, because the God of love has filled my heart. May all who read this testimony of my life find His amazing love filling them too. May Jesus, who is longing for you, pick you up even now! May you feel His loving arms, carrying you across the threshold that is now before you. May you live out the rest of your days in the place you belong...going out with Him, into the world.

I am available for Encountering Christ Within seminars to impart what is found in these pages. I have spoken at churches, pastor's conferences, women's retreats and Aglow meetings. I would love to have you invite me to come and speak where you are as well, but only if it is His Voice you have heard while reading. Jesus is the Living Word, and He alone has the words of life.

The desire of my heart in writing this book is for you to know the desire of His. His desire is for you. He wants you to be with Him where He is. This book is to be like an escort to take you personally into His Presence. To order copies of this book, and for scheduling dates please contact me at **debracossu@ihop.org** or **dlcossu@gmail.com** or at my web site **www.longing4you.**com There you will find information concerning seminars and retreats, the lifestyle of Encountering Christ Within, my newsletters and help for those going through the various stages of life loss and grief recovery.

Please feel free to email any prayer requests you would like me to pray about with you. We have prayer requests that come in from all over the world, and I will gladly put yours into the basket where it is prayed for by the staff missionaries who also serve in that area. You can now visit the prayer room by watching Direct TV channel 365, or go to www. god.tv for online access.

I am inviting those who have been blessed reading this book, and who are able to partner with me in my missionary efforts here in the House of Prayer, to join my support team. Simply let me know you are interested, and I will contact you personally.

Copies of my book can also be ordered from the www. ihop.org online bookstore, as well as through Amazon, and Barnes & Noble. For tax-deductible donations, please make checks payable to "IHOP-KC" keeping the memo blank, and include a sticky note that it is support for Debra Cossu.

I would also love to hear of the impact this book has had on your heart.

Mail support to:

> Debra Cossu
> 11112 Applewood Drive
> Kansas City, MO 64134